Why Schools Fail

Why Schools Fail

BRUCE GOLDBERG

Washington, D.C.

Library of Congress Cataloging-in-Publication Data

Goldberg, Bruce, 1937–
    Why schools fail / Bruce Goldberg.   p.   cm.
    Includes bibliographical references (p.   ) and index.
    ISBN 1-882577-39-6. — ISBN 1-882577-40-X (pbk.)
    1. Education—Aims and Objectives—United States.   2. Education—
United States—Philosophy.   3. Education change—United States.
I. Title
LA212.G64   1996
370'.973—dc21   96-39244
                                                                 CIP

Cover Design by Mark Fondersmith.

Printed in the United States of America.

CATO INSTITUTE
1000 Massachusetts Ave., N.W.
Washington, D.C. 20001

To the memory of my mother

Gloria Goldberg

Human nature is not a machine to be built after a model, and set to do exactly the work prescribed for it, but a tree, which requires to grow and develop itself on all sides, according to the tendency of the inward forces which make it a living thing.

John Stuart Mill, On Liberty

Contents

ACKNOWLEDGMENTS   xi

INTRODUCTION   1

1. IS EDUCATIONAL THEORY SCIENTIFIC?   5

2. EDUCATIONAL RHETORIC VS. SCHOOL REALITY   27

3. THE BASICS: MATHEMATICS   35

4. THE BASICS: READING   43

5. WHY EDUCATIONAL REFORMS HAVE FAILED   63

6. ON MEMORIZING   79

7. SHAPING HUMAN BEINGS AND PSEUDOSCIENCE   85

8. EDUCATION AND INDIVIDUAL CHOICE   95

SELECTED BIBLIOGRAPHY   115

INDEX   121

Acknowledgments

I would like to thank Robert Nozick for many illuminating philosophical discussions and, in particular, for the discussion that led me to think about schooling. My thanks also to Linda Goldberg and Rick Bryan for their enthusiasm and encouragement. I am most deeply grateful to Sharon Scott, whose heart and mind made the writing of this book possible.

Introduction

In 1959 James B. Conant, former president of Harvard, writing about the American school system, said, "It works, most of us like it, and it appears to be as permanent a feature of our society as most of our political institutions."[1] Given the widespread support for public schooling, there are probably not many people who would quarrel with the observation that the institution is permanent. Today, however, many people might hold that Conant somewhat overstated the case for his first two claims. For if there are those who do like the public school system, there are also many who do not. Dissatisfaction with schooling is widespread at all levels. Among high school students the dropout rate is 25 percent. A third of all new teachers leave the teaching profession after two years. Every day more than a million children are required to take psychoactive drugs so that their behavior in school will be "manageable."

Facts like those have led some observers to conclude that if the system can be said to be working, it is doing so very poorly. Within 10 years of Conant's optimistic study of high schools, there were calls for a complete restructuring, or even abandonment, of formal education, and the bestseller list featured such titles as *Crisis in the Classroom*, *The Underachieving School*, and *Deschooling Society*. The central question raised by those and other works was, Why is the system not working in anything like the way intended?

What seems undeniable is that there is a substantial contrast between the vision of what public education is supposed to be and the reality of schooling itself. Educators have tended to portray schooling in glowing terms. Horace Mann, the "father" of the public school system in America, claimed that the process of schooling would "build up the nature of the child into a capacity for the intellectual comprehension of the universe and a spiritual similitude

---

[1] James B. Conant, *The American High School Today* (New York: Signet Books, 1959), p. 19.

1

to its Author."[2] As a result of going to school, children would acquire "the bloom and elasticity of perfect health, manners born of artlessness and enthusiasm, and a countenance so inscribed with the records of pure thoughts and benevolent deeds, as to be one beaming, holy hieroglyph of love and duty."[3]

It is difficult to escape the conclusion that the schools have fallen somewhat short of achieving that vision. As many observers have seen them, they are not the benevolent, beneficial places Mann envisioned. Schools are often, in effect if not in intent, rather dreadful places in which to spend time. Charles Silberman, then an editor of *Fortune* magazine, wrote in *Crisis in the Classroom,*

> It is not possible to spend any prolonged period visiting public school classrooms without being appalled by the mutilation visible everywhere—mutilation of spontaneity, of joy in learning, of pleasure in creating, of sense of self. The public schools . . . are the kind of institution one cannot really dislike until one gets to know them well. Because adults take the schools so much for granted, they fail to appreciate what grim, joyless places most American schools are, how oppressive and petty are the rules by which they are governed, how intellectually and esthetically barren the atmosphere.[4]

When critics characterize the failure of schooling in terms of the mutilation of the child's sense of self or the suppression of the child's individuality, as opposed to declining Scholastic Aptitude Test scores, defenders of the status quo tend to react with derision. They see such criticisms as expressions of "naive romanticism" or "romantic individualism." A child's education, they say, is to be directed by educational professionals, implementing the knowledge they have gained from their study of educational science, that is, knowledge of the conditions required for children's optimal mental growth. Education is not to be left to the subjective intuitions of romantic dreamers with their foolish ideas about children being the best judges of what they need to know or being allowed to do whatever they want to do.

---

[2]Horace Mann, *Lectures and Annual Reports on Education,* ed. Mary Mann (Cambridge, Mass.: Published for the editor, 1867), p. 227.

[3]Ibid., p. 220.

[4]Charles Silberman, *Crisis in the Classroom* (New York: Random House, 1970), p. 10.

There are, I believe, two things wrong with that response. First, the claims educators have made to scientific knowledge of what children require do not sustain examination. To put the point more strongly, there is no such thing as educational science. When the views that have been offered as scientific are examined closely, they turn out to be not scientific at all but rather a combination of personal taste and simplistic, distorted versions of philosophical theories about how the mind works. Second, the denial of children's individuality is not to be taken lightly. What careful observation of children actually shows is that great harm is done when there is a systematic suppression of a child's interests, values, and idiosyncratic potentials. Indeed, it is the denial of individuality, the idea that everyone must follow some general plan, that is at the core of the failure of the schools.

In brief, defenders of schooling in its present form claim that its programs are arrived at scientifically and are applicable to everyone. I believe that the programs are not arrived at scientifically and are not applicable to everyone. The present work is an attempt to illustrate those points.

1. Is Educational Theory Scientific?

Horace Mann was one of the first educators to claim that the process of formal schooling is based on scientific knowledge of how a child's mind develops. Without that knowledge, he said, one would have no right "to attempt to manage and direct ... a child's soul."[1] Given that Mann is praised by contemporary educators for his insight and for the "modernism" of his views,[2] it is somewhat disconcerting to discover that the science that he saw as guiding the process of schooling was phrenology, the now entirely discredited pseudoscience of bumps on the skull. The book he regarded as containing the knowledge necessary for training children's minds was *The Constitution of Man* by the Scottish phrenologist George Combe. "Its philosophy," Mann said, "is the only practical basis for education."[3]

Combe held that the mind consisted of some 30 faculties or "propensities," such as benevolence, combativeness, self-esteem, and veneration. Each of those faculties was located in a particular part of the brain. As the faculty developed, the area of the brain in which it was located got larger, pushing out the skull. Using that "scientific" knowledge, one could cultivate the desirable faculties and suppress the undesirable ones by using an objective method, that is, by measuring the "bumps" on the skull to determine how well the process was proceeding.

The Behaviorists

The claim that schooling is guided by scientific knowledge has been made by countless educators, but it has never been supported by any evidence. Just as Mann thought that phrenology provided

[1]Horace Mann, *Lectures and Annual Reports on Education*, ed. Mary Mann (Cambridge, Mass.: Published for the editor, 1867), p. 223.

[2]Lawrence A. Cremin, "Horace Mann's Legacy," in *The Republic and the School*, ed. Lawrence A. Cremin (New York: Teachers College, Columbia, 1957), p. 16.

[3]Quoted in Jonathan Messerli, *Horace Mann: A Biography* (New York: Alfred A. Knopf, 1972), p. 351.

the scientific basis for training children's minds, many educators in this century believed they had found the key in behaviorist psychology.

It has become clear, however, that the behaviorist psychologists, in claiming to have a scientific understanding of human mental development and a scientific foundation for schooling, vastly overstated their case. Their claims were nothing if not grand. One of the leading behaviorists, Clark Hull, said that on the basis of psychological laws, stated entirely in terms of stimuli and responses, he would provide a scientific explanation of "familial behavior, individual adaptive efficiency (intelligence), the formal educative processes, psychogenic disorders, social control and delinquency, character and personality, culture and acculturation, magic and religious practices, custom, law and jurisprudence, politics and government."[4] Hull's actual achievement was somewhat more modest. It consisted, as the philosopher R. S. Peters pointed out, of nothing but "some simple postulates which gave dubious answers to limited questions about particular species of rats."[5]

Behaviorism has been the most influential psychological theory among educators in the present century. The theory, originally advanced by Johns Hopkins psychologist John B. Watson in 1913, claimed to place psychology, for the first time, on a scientific foundation.[6] For psychology to become a genuine science alongside physics and biology, Watson argued, it was necessary to abandon the concepts and methods of the discipline as it had been practiced up till then. According to the traditional, so-called introspective or mentalistic view, psychology was the study of mental states and processes, such as consciousness in general, thinking, remembering, having an intention, desiring, and willing. Its goal was to discover the nature of those processes and the laws governing their causal interactions. The principal method of investigation was introspection. By carefully attending to what actually took place in the mind when he or she thought or remembered and so on, the perceptive psychologist could

---

[4]Clark L. Hull, *Principles of Behavior* (New York: Appleton-Century-Crofts, 1943), p. 399.

[5]R. S. Peters, *The Concept of Motivation* (London: Routledge & Kegan Paul, 1958), p. 3.

[6]John B. Watson, "Psychology As the Behaviorist Views It," *Psychological Review* 20 (March 1913): 158–77.

discover important truths about what is involved in mental functioning. In addition, the psychologist could use as data the reports of subjects asked to describe their own mental experiences. William James's *Principles of Psychology,* a widely read work of the time, illustrated the introspective approach. In his chapter on "The Stream of Thought," for example, James described in great detail how the different parts of a thought ebb and flow as the thought passes through the mind.

Watson's contention was that introspection is unreliable and unscientific. It is unreliable in that introspective reports vary widely from individual to individual. It is unscientific in that reports of subjective experiences are, by their very nature, unverifiable. Watson argued further that the data gathered by introspective methods did not enable psychologists to predict behavior.

The alternative to introspectionism is for psychology to focus on what is objectively observable, namely, how organisms behave in response to stimuli. For several years Watson experimented on rats learning to run mazes. He concluded that, in terms of the concepts of "stimulus, response, habit formation, habit integration and the like," one can fully explain how animals learn and how they acquire their repertoire of behavior.[7]

The fundamental explanatory concept in accounting for both animal and human behavior was the conditioned reflex. The Russian physiologist Ivan Pavlov had shown that animal responses could be "conditioned." If one paired a stimulus, such as a bell, with food, a dog's natural salivary response to food would soon be evoked by the bell alone. The bell became a conditioned stimulus and salivation a conditioned response.

Watson conducted a series of experiments on conditioned responses in human beings. He was able to show that, by pairing a sound with an electric shock, people could be conditioned to fear the sound alone. The goal of psychology, he held, was to provide laws describing such stimulus-response connections for human behavior in general. Then, "given the stimulus, psychology can predict what the response will be; or, on the other hand, given the response, it can predict the nature of the effective stimulus."[8] In

[7]Ibid., p. 167.

[8]John B. Watson, "An Attempted Formulation of the Scope of Behavior Psychology," *Psychological Review* 24 (September 1917): 333.

possession of such laws, the psychologist would have a technology of behavior control. "Behaviorism states frankly," Watson said, "that its goal is the gathering of facts necessary to enable it to predict and to control human behavior."[9]

Over the next two decades Watson wrote numerous articles and books describing the social and educational implications of the new science of human behavior. Not only in scholarly journals such as *Psychological Review*, but also in such mass-circulation magazines as *Harper's*, the *New Republic*, the *Saturday Review*, and *McCall's*, Watson expressed views on a wide variety of topics: the nature of marriage; how to raise children; the origin of fears; and the usefulness of psychology in prisons, in schools, and for directing society generally.

The central idea throughout was that, since a human being is "nothing but an organic machine," we are able "to predict that machine's behavior and to control it as we do other machines."[10] Viewed in that way, psychology had great social utility. It could provide, Watson said, "laws and principles whereby man's actions can be controlled by organized society.... If it is demanded by society that a given line of conduct is desirable, the psychologist should be able with some certainty to arrange the situation or factors which will lead the individual most quickly and with the least expenditure of effort to perform that task."[11]

Watson recommended that child psychologists, in possession of behaviorist techniques, take over the early years of schooling so that "many of the mishaps to the emotions due to home training could be corrected." And he added, "We could certainly be sure that from their entrance into the school system of our country no further mistakes would occur."[12]

[9]*New School for Social Research Announcement (1922–1923)*, p. 9, quoted in Kerry W. Buckley, *Mechanical Man: John Broadus Watson and the Beginnings of Behaviorism* (New York: Guilford, 1989), p. 155.

[10]John B. Watson, "Influencing the Mind of Another," Speech delivered to the Montreal Advertising Club, September 26, 1934, quoted in Buckley, p. 137.

[11]John B. Watson, *Psychology from the Standpoint of a Behaviorist* (Philadelphia: J. B. Lippincott, 1919), p. vii; see also John B. Watson, "Practical and Theoretical Problems in Instinct and Habit," in *Suggestions of Modern Science Concerning Education*, ed. H. S. Jennings et al. (New York: Macmillan, 1917), p. 82.

[12]Ibid., p. 76.

Watson's ideas were widely discussed and highly praised. Reviewing his 1924 book, *Behaviorism,* the *New York Times* said that Watson had inaugurated "a new epoch in the intellectual history of man."[13] The *Herald Tribune* went further: "This is perhaps the most important book ever written. One stands for an instant blinded by a great hope."[14] Bertrand Russell, though he expressed reservations concerning its authoritarianism, said that Watson's work constituted the most important achievement in psychology since Aristotle.[15]

The enthusiasm was misplaced. Over the years, scrutiny has shown that both Watson's experimental techniques and his supposedly scientific theorizing were seriously flawed. His claim that behaviorism constituted a science of human behavior was unjustified.

In 1920 Watson reported on a study that has become one of the most discussed psychological experiments in the history of the discipline. It is, as one writer put it, "the classic illustration of conditioning in the folklore of psychology."[16] While some commentators found the experiment morally repugnant, many saw it as a dramatic demonstration of the validity of the behaviorist approach.

The experiment involved producing conditioned fear in an infant. The child, Albert B., had been raised from birth in a hospital where his mother worked. He was nine months old when the experiment began.

Watson's first goal was to establish that Albert had no fear of a variety of objects. The child was confronted successively with a white rat, a rabbit, a dog, a monkey, masks with and without hair, cotton wool, and burning newspapers. Watson notes, with emphasis, *"At no time did this infant show fear in any situation."*[17]

It was next determined that Albert would show fear if startled by a loud noise. While his assistant occupied Albert's attention, Watson, standing behind the child, struck a hammer against a suspended

[13]*New York Times,* August 2, 1925, quoted in Buckley, p. 173.

[14]*New York Herald Tribune,* June 21, 1925, quoted in ibid.

[15]David Cohen, *J. B. Watson: The Founder of Behaviorism* (London: Routledge & Kegan Paul, 1979), p. 2.

[16]Buckley, p. 121.

[17]John B. Watson and Rosalie Rayner, "Conditioned Emotional Reactions," *Journal of Experimental Psychology* 3 (1920): 1–14. All quotations concerning what took place during the experiment are from this article.

steel bar. "The child started violently, his breathing was checked and the arms were raised in a characteristic manner." When the bar was struck a second time, the same thing occurred, and "in addition the lips began to pucker and tremble." The third time, Albert "broke into a sudden crying fit."

Two months later, the conditioning of fear began. The white rat was taken out of a basket and presented to Albert. As soon as he touched the rat, the steel bar was struck. "The infant jumped violently and fell forward, burying his face in the mattress. He did not cry, however." When Albert touched the rat a second time, the bar was struck again. "Again the infant jumped violently, fell forward and began to whimper." It was decided at that point to halt the experiment for a week "in order not to disturb the child too seriously."

The effects of the experience were still observable after a week. When he was presented with the rat, Albert reached out tentatively, but "when the rat nosed the infant's left hand, the hand was immediately withdrawn." Albert began to reach out again but pulled back before any contact was made. Watson then continued to experiment on Albert in a series of steps that he described as follows:

> 2. Joint stimulation with rat and sound. Started, then fell over immediately to the right side. No crying.
> 3. Joint stimulation. Fell to right side and rested upon hands, with head turned away from rat. No crying.
> 4. Joint stimulation. Same reaction.
> 5. Rat suddenly presented alone. Puckered face, whimpered and withdrew body sharply to the left.
> 6. Joint stimulation. Fell over immediately to right side and began to whimper.
> 7. Joint stimulation. Started violently and cried, but did not fall over.
> 8. Rat alone. *The instant the rat was shown the baby began to cry. Almost instantly he turned sharply to the left, fell over on left side, raised himself on all fours and began to crawl away so rapidly that he was caught with difficulty before reaching the edge of the table.*

Watson's conclusion, at the close of the first phase of the experiment, was that "this was as convincing a case of a completely conditioned fear response as could have been theoretically pictured."

The next goal, pursued five days later, was to find out whether Albert's fear would transfer to other objects. A rabbit was put in front of him. "He leaned as far away from the animal as possible, whimpered, then burst into tears." When the rabbit was placed in contact with him, "he buried his face in the mattress, then got up on all fours and crawled away, crying as he went." Watson remarks that that was "a most convincing test." Next tried was a dog, which "did not produce as violent a reaction as the rabbit." The dog was followed by a sealskin coat. Albert "began to fret." When the coat was put close to him, "he turned immediately, began to cry and tried to crawl away on all fours." That was followed by cotton wool, which "he kicked . . . away but did not touch . . . with his hands." Then, "just in play," Watson put his head down to see if Albert would play with his hair. The reaction was "completely negative." Finally, a Santa Claus mask was presented, to which Albert was "pronouncedly negative."

The next aim was to see if Albert's responses would be different if the environment were changed, so it was decided to move the experiment to a larger room. Before moving, though, Watson "thought it best . . . to freshen the reaction both to the rabbit and to the dog by showing them at the moment the steel bar was struck." In both cases, when the steel bar was struck, Albert's fear reaction was described as "violent."

In the larger room, when the rabbit was presented, Albert "turned to the left and kept his face away from the animal but the reaction was never pronounced." When the dog was brought in he cried. His "hands moved as far away from the animal as possible. Whimpered as long as the dog was present." The rat caused only a slight negative reaction. So "it was thought best to freshen the reaction to the rat. The sound was given just as the rat was presented. Albert jumped violently but did not cry." When the rat was then presented alone, Albert reacted by "drawing back his body, raising his hands, whimpering, etc." The rabbit was then presented again. "Pronounced reaction. Whimpered with arms held high, fell over backward and had to be caught." Then the dog was brought in again. At first it did not produce much of a reaction. But then the dog barked loudly three times six inches from Albert's face. "Albert immediately fell over and broke into a wail that continued until the dog was removed." Watson adds that "the sudden barking of the

11

hitherto quiet dog produced a marked fear response in the adult observers!"

The final aim was to determine how long Albert's fears would persist. After 31 days, during which no further tests were conducted, the objects were again presented. To varying degrees, Albert continued to show fear.

Watson described that experiment in several of his writings, citing it in support of a variety of claims about how the emotions develop, how habits are acquired, and how human beings learn. In addition, it was offered as a demonstration of a procedure for achieving what he had declared to be the major behaviorist goal: "bringing the human emotions under experimental control."[18] Watson's analysis of the experiment was widely accepted. It remains one of the most frequently cited experiments in textbooks of developmental and abnormal psychology. However, as several critics have noted, Watson's experiment on Albert, as a scientific investigation or a scientific demonstration, was deficient.

The experiment involved one subject and the conditioning of one emotion. And there was no follow-up. Given those methodological flaws, the experiment could not go very far toward establishing anything, certainly not Watson's claim that he had demonstrated a technique for conditioning human emotions "at will."[19] Indeed, when one investigator conducted a modified version of Watson's experiment, using a disagreeable noise, she found it impossible to condition even 1 of 15 children to fear wooden and cloth objects.[20]

The idea that any emotional and behavioral characteristics can be imposed on a child "at will" was the linchpin of Watson's theory. It was what lay behind his claim that, using conditioning techniques, psychology could produce human beings to order. "It lies easily within our control," he said, "to perfect and regulate and reshape and use practically the emotional life of the individual."[21] Somewhat more dramatically, he claimed,

---

[18]John B. Watson and J. J. B. Morgan, "Emotional Reactions and Psychological Experimentation," *American Journal of Psychology* 28 (1917): 174.

[19]Ibid., p. 171.

[20]E. O. Bregman, "An Attempt to Modify the Emotional Attitudes of Children by the Conditioned Response Technique," *Journal of Genetic Psychology* 45 (1934): 169–98.

[21]Watson, "Practical and Theoretical Problems in Instinct and Habit," p. 57.

> Give me a dozen healthy infants, well formed, and my
> own specified world to bring them up in and I'll guarantee
> to take any one at random and train him to become any type
> of specialist I might select—doctor, lawyer, artist, merchant-
> chief and yes, even beggar-man, thief, regardless of his tal-
> ents, penchants, tendencies, abilities, vocations, and race of
> his ancestors.[22]

Watson's actual accomplishments were considerably less substantial. Before the experiment on Albert, he had merely been able to
produce a conditioned fear response in a small group of subjects by
pairing a tone with an electric shock. And he had had only partial
success. Certain of the subjects in his early experiments, he reported,
failed to develop a conditioned fear response even when he turned
up the current so that the electric shock was "strong enough to
induce perspiration."[23]

More important, though, is that Watson was mistaken in his idea
that training can be carried out without regard for a person's (or
any organism's) innate endowment and propensities. The central
role of that claim in behaviorist learning theory has led to its receiving considerable attention from psychologists over the years. There
now exists a substantial body of experimental literature showing
that efforts to condition animals against their natural propensities,
after some limited initial success, are soon overwhelmed by those
natural propensities. The attempts run up against what one study
calls "instinctive drift."[24]

Even Albert's behavior did not conform to Watson's conclusions.
Though that can be seen in his own account, it escaped his attention.
Albert did have some extreme fear responses, but his behavior was
not uniform, and he had other responses that cannot be characterized
as fear. For example, on one occasion when the rat was presented,
Albert crawled away, but without the terror he had shown at other
times. "There was no crying, but strange to say, as he started away

[22]John B. Watson, *Behaviorism* (1924; Chicago: University of Chicago Press, 1961),
p. 104.

[23]John B. Watson, "The Place of the Conditioned Reflex in Psychology," *Psychological
Review* 23 (March 1916): 97.

[24]Keller Breland and Marian Breland, "The Misbehavior of Organisms," in *Biological
Boundaries of Learning*, ed. Martin E. P. Seligman and Joanne L. Hager (New York:
Appleton-Century-Crofts, 1972), p. 185.

he began to gurgle and coo, even while leaning far over to the left side to avoid the rat." And though Albert was "completely negative" when invited to play with Watson's hair, he "immediately began to play" with the hair of two observers who did the same thing. Though he first kicked away the cotton wool, he wound up touching it after all. As Watson put it, Albert, "under the influence of the manipulative instinct, lost some of his negativism to the wool." And after the 31-day break he actually initiated contact with the rabbit. "After about a minute he reached out tentatively and slowly and touched the rabbit's ear with his right hand, finally manipulating it."

The carelessness in Watson's thinking is not confined to the experiment on Albert. Carelessness pervades behaviorist theory. The most fundamental concepts are carelessly drawn, calling the entire framework into question. For example, the concept of a behavioral response is defined in two quite different ways. In many places Watson describes responses as consisting of such things as "muscle contractions and gland secretions."[25] In other places he offers a quite different notion: "By response we mean anything the animal does— such as turning toward or away from a light, jumping at a sound, and more highly organized activities such as building a skyscraper, drawing plans, having babies, writing books, and the like."[26]

Watson glosses over a distinction that is of great importance, the distinction between purely physiological responses and purposive human action. The psychologist Edward Chace Tolman observed in this connection,

> Watson has in reality dallied with two different notions of behavior, though he himself has not clearly seen how different they are. On the one hand, he has defined behavior in terms of its strict underlying physical and physiological details, i.e., in terms of receptor-process, conductor-process, and effector-process per se. . . . And, on the other hand, he has come to recognize, albeit perhaps but dimly, that behavior, as such, is more than and different from the sum of its physiological parts. Behavior, as such, is an "emergent" phenomenon that has descriptive and defining properties of its own.[27]

[25]John B. Watson, *Psychology from the Standpoint of a Behaviorist* (Philadelphia: J. B. Lippincott, 1919), p. 10.

[26]Watson, *Behaviorism*, p. 5.

[27]Edward Chace Tolman, *Purposive Behavior in Animals and Men* (New York: Appleton-Century-Crofts, 1932), pp. 6–7.

The distinction between those two concepts of behavior is important because understanding behavior in the second sense involves just those ideas that behaviorism rules out, ideas such as belief, intention, and purpose. As Tolman put it, "Behavior as behavior reeks of purpose and cognition."[28]

In spite of its failings, behaviorism attracted a considerable following, both in and out of the academic world. Watson was invited numerous times to give talks on the radio. On one nationwide NBC broadcast, for example, he spoke on "how to grow a personality." He was the subject of a profile in the *New Yorker*. In the academic world, behaviorism became *the* scientific approach for many psychologists and educators. As one dissenter noted, with regret, "Behaviorism has spread over the country in a great wave."[29]

In 1928 Watson, together with his wife Rosalie Rayner Watson (who had been his assistant in the Albert experiment), published *Psychological Care of Infant and Child*. That, too, was received with enthusiasm, selling over 100,000 copies within a few months.[30] The popularity of the work is puzzling, since Watson's advice about how to behave toward one's children is not much more heartwarming than the experiment on Albert.

> Never hug and kiss them, never let them sit on your lap. If you must, kiss them once on the forehead when they say goodnight. Shake hands with them in the morning. Give them a pat on the head if they have made an extraordinarily good job of a difficult task. Try it out. In a week's time you will find how easy it is to be perfectly objective with your child and at the same time kindly. You will be utterly ashamed of the mawkish, sentimental way you have been handling it.[31]

Watson's granddaughter, actress Mariette Hartley, in her autobiography, *Breaking the Silence*, describes the devastating effect that approach had on Watson's own children. Fortunately, his children

[28]Ibid., p. 7.

[29]E. B. Titchener, letter to G. Tschelpanow, October 25, 1924, quoted in Buckley, p. 150.

[30]Cohen, p. 217.

[31]John B. Watson and Rosalie R. Watson, *Psychological Care of Infant and Child* (New York: W. W. Norton, 1928), pp. 81–82.

were spared the implementation of some of his other ideas about child training, his idea about teaching children to "let objects alone," for example. "Would it not be possible," he wrote, "to arrange a table containing interesting but not to be touched objects with electric wires so that an electrical shock is given when the table to be avoided is touched?"[32]

Behaviorism gained strength in Watson's wake, reaching its greatest popularity with the writings of B. F. Skinner, perhaps the most influential psychologist of the century. Like Watson, Skinner claimed to be in possession of a scientific theory of human behavior with far-reaching social and educational implications. But Skinner's formulations turned out to be no more carefully crafted than Watson's. If anything, Skinner's work reveals even more clearly the poverty of behaviorism as a psychological theory. As with Watson, the difficulties concern, not this or that detail, but the fundamental concepts and principles of the system.

There is, for example, the fundamental law that Skinner calls "the law of conditioning." It says, "If the occurrence of [a response] is followed by presence of a reinforcing stimulus, the strength is increased."[33] Reinforcement is explained in this way: "The operation of reinforcement is defined as the presentation of a certain kind of stimulus in a temporal relation with either a stimulus or response. A reinforcing stimulus is defined as such by its power to produce the resulting change [in strength]."[34] As several commentators have pointed out, given that definition of the notion of reinforcement, the "law of conditioning" is not a scientific law at all but an empty tautology. Noam Chomsky, in his review of Skinner's *Verbal Behavior*, states, "The term is used in such a way that the assertion that reinforcement is necessary for learning and continued availability of behavior is . . . empty."[35]

Similar problems arise in connection with Skinner's attempts to explain some specific aspect of human behavior. He attempts to

[32]John B. Watson, letter to Patty S. Hill, August 1, 1923, quoted in Buckley, p. 153.

[33]B. F. Skinner, *The Behavior of Organisms* (New York: Appleton-Century-Crofts, 1938), p. 21.

[34]Ibid., p. 62.

[35]Noam Chomsky, "A Review of B. F. Skinner's *Verbal Behavior*," in *The Structure of Language: Readings in the Philosophy of Language*, ed. Jerry A. Fodor and Jerrold J. Katz (Englewood Cliffs, N.J.: Prentice-Hall, 1964), p. 557.

offer an explanation of why people respond as they do to what he calls "aversive stimulation," threats, for example. One explains a response to a threat, he says, in terms of the person's history of reinforcement. If the person has had a history of appropriate reinforcement, then he will give the appropriate response to the threat. As Skinner puts it, if a certain response in the past was followed by "cessation of the threat of such injury—of events which have previously been followed by such injury and which are therefore conditioned aversive stimuli," then the person will give that response.[36] But that formulation leads to absurdity. As Chomsky notes, "It would appear to follow from this description that a [person] will not respond properly to the [threat] *Your money or your life* unless he has a past history of being killed."[37]

But even if the formulation were repaired so as not to yield that absurdity, the attempt to account for human behavior in terms of conditioning would not get off the ground. Suppose someone is threatened with "Your money or your life" and responds by handing over his wallet. The explanation of that action cannot be that he has been conditioned to act that way since, let us suppose, this is the first time he has been in that situation. His response, handing over his wallet to the man with the gun, is one he has never made before. The philosopher Daniel Dennett comments,

> The Skinnerian must claim that this is not truly novel behavior at all, but an instance of a general sort of behavior which has been previously conditioned. But what sort is it? Not only have I not been trained to hand over my wallet to men with guns, I have not been trained to empty my pockets for women with bombs, nor to turn over my possessions to armed entities. I may never have been threatened before at all. Or more plausibly, it may well be that most often when I have been threatened in the past, the "reinforced" response was to *apologize* to the threatener for something I'd said. Obviously, though, when told "Your money or your life!" I don't respond by saying, "I'm sorry. I take it all back."[38]

The point is that the explanation of why the person hands over his wallet is that he believes that he will be killed if he doesn't, that he

[36]Skinner, p. 33.

[37]Chomsky, p. 566.

[38]Daniel C. Dennett, "Skinner Skinned," in *Brainstorms: Philosophical Essays on Mind and Psychology* (Cambridge, Mass.: Bradford Books, 1978), p. 67.

wants to stay alive, and that he is rational. But, as noted earlier, those concepts, of belief, desire, purpose, and so on, lie outside the behaviorist framework.

Like Watson, Skinner carelessly generalized from quite limited laboratory results. It turned out, for example, that pigeons can be conditioned, in a short time, to walk around holding their heads above a given height. That, and similar pigeon behavior, is well explained in terms of schedules of reinforcement. But it is a mistake to conclude that human action can be understood in terms of such a simple model. Skinner tended to lose sight of the fact that, as Dennett put it, "pigeons do not exhibit very interesting novel behavior, but human beings do."[39]

The goal of the behaviorists, Watson, Hull, Skinner, and many others, was a theory of learning—and of human psychology in general—based on a few principles concerning conditioned responses, principles derived largely from experiments on animals. But the principles that are provided, even when they are themselves not crippled by self-contradiction, don't begin to capture the richness and subtlety of the phenomena they seek to explain.

Why then did so many educators embrace behaviorist psychology? The main reason, I believe, is that they saw behaviorist theory as giving scientific legitimacy to their enterprise. They thought they had found in behaviorism what Horace Mann thought he had found in phrenology, a scientific justification for the practices of schooling.

Though behaviorism still has supporters, their number is dwindling rapidly. One observer of the current scene writes, "The interest of psychologists in animal learning theory is on the wane. Although the reasons are many, a prominent one is that such theories have failed to capture and bring into the laboratory phenomena which provide fertile models of complex human learning."[40]

The history of educational theorizing is littered with false claims to scientific knowledge. It is not possible to examine every such theory, to show how it is wrong and how it fails to serve the interests of children, but it may be useful to look somewhat more closely at one current effort.

---

[39]Ibid.

[40]Martin E. P. Seligman, "On the Generality of the Laws of Learning," *Psychological Review* 77, no. 5 (1970): 414.

Jean Piaget

In recent years the attention of many educators has turned to the work of the Swiss psychologist Jean Piaget. Once again it is being claimed that a well-confirmed scientific theory has been provided, placing schooling on a solid foundation. Schooling in the past, it is held, because it was based on false psychological theories, was indeed arbitrary, misguided, and harmful to children. That supposedly has been changed by Piaget's work. Many programs have been established, in various parts of the world, for training children according to techniques derived from Piaget's theory.

Is the new approach justified? Can it produce a real transformation of schooling based on verified scientific knowledge about human mental development? A look at the facts, unfortunately, does not provide much reason for optimism.

It is not easy to say very clearly what Piaget's theory is. As even his most ardent followers are quick to point out, his presentation of the theory is often quite dense, his style of writing tortuous. In addition, there are many inconsistencies in his account, allowing for incompatible interpretations, each of which may be justified by pointing to the text. But, in broad outline, the following may be said.

Piaget's theory, which he describes as a "genetic epistemology," concerns the development in human beings of "rational" or "logical" thought, which is referred to as "fundamental intelligence." According to the theory, fundamental intelligence develops in four stages:

Sensory-motor thinking (birth to age 2)
Preoperational thinking (age 2 to age 7)
Concrete operations (age 7 to age 11)
Formal operations (age 11 and older)

It is in the fourth stage that fully developed rational thinking appears, when the principles of "propositional logic" are mastered. Before that time, the thought of the child is illogical. "Before the age of ten or eleven the child is hardly capable of any kind of formal reasoning."[41] The central task of schooling, according to that view, is to facilitate the development of logical thinking by introducing the child, as early as possible, to the main concepts of propositional

---

[41]Jean Piaget, *Science of Education and the Psychology of the Child* (New York: Orion, 1970), p. 163.

logic such as class inclusion, logical addition, and logical multiplication.

Let us look at the theory in action. The following is a transcript from a film intended to demonstrate the utility of teaching based on Piaget's theory. The film was prepared by the Nuffield Mathematics Project and was shown on the BBC. In one scene a teacher and a boy of about six or seven are standing in front of a table. On the table are three tulips and six daisies.

> TEACHER: Are there more flowers or daisies?
> CHILD: More daisies.
> T: More daisies. Right. Now, I'm just wondering whether there aren't more flowers, because the daisies are part of the flowers. That's right, isn't it?
> C: Yes.
> T: And the tulips are also part of the flowers?
> C: . . .(Does not reply)
> T: Is that right?
> C: Yes.
> T: And so the whole lot of them are flowers. Now, I think they're all flowers but only these ones [pointing] are daisies. So I think there are more flowers than daisies.
> C: . . .
> T: Now, does that make sense?
> C: . . . [After a long pause] No.
> T: [With a chuckle] Are there more flowers or more daisies?
> C: More daisies.
> T: More daisies.
> COMMENTATOR: Who would imagine that this is the child's view of the world?[42]

There is a great deal in that exchange that one might find disconcerting. There is the patronizing tone of the adult, the stiffness and the emotional distance between the participants, the fact that the child is being thoroughly confused and bewildered. John Holt, the pioneering critic of schooling, goes so far as to call the scene "almost sinister."[43] At the least, it does not seem to be an insightful or helpful way of dealing with a child.

---

[42]Quoted in John Holt, *The Underachieving School* (New York: Dell, 1972), p. 68.
[43]Ibid., p. 69.

But is insight involved here nevertheless? Is there, in spite of the apparent emptiness of the "discussion," something valuable taking place?

Consider the conclusion being drawn by the commentator, that the child is demonstrating illogical thinking. He is incapable, it is held, of grasping a simple truth involving the concept of class inclusion; he cannot deal with part-whole relationships. He is unable to see that if one class of things, A (daisies), is part of another class of things, B (flowers), then there are more Bs than there are As. That is part of what Piaget is referring to when he says that such a child is "incapable of handling propositional logic."

It would seem, however, that that is not an accurate description of the child's difficulty. One can see that the interview consists of a highly artificial, and unequal, exchange in which the child is altogether ill at ease. As so often happens in school, he is not so much thinking about the matter at hand as he is trying to give the answer he believes the teacher wants. And does the child even understand the question he is being asked? I think he does not, and with good reason. The question "Are there more daisies or flowers" is unnatural and confusing. In virtually every life situation in which one is asked to compare two groups of things, A and B, it is not the case, as it is here, that A is a subclass of B. One is asked, "Are there more cups or saucers?" "Are there more cars or trucks?" "More men or women?" but not "Are there more blue cups or cups?" "More trucks or vehicles?" "More men or people?"

Holt writes, "When I first read about Piaget's part-whole experiments, it seemed likely to me that, regardless of what they had been told, the children were in fact comparing one part of the class (of beads or flowers or whatever) with the part that was left. That was the kind of comparison they were used to making, and indeed the only one that seemed to make any sense."[44] The child's response is not an illogical one. He is attempting to make sense of the question asked. When that attempt results in disapproval and ridicule, he is left confused and bewildered. What is going on, then, is that a false theory has produced an artificial, unnatural use of language that, in turn, results in the thwarting of a natural response.

[44]Ibid.

But, it may be asked further, Why is this taking place at all? Why is the child being asked questions intended to focus on his supposed incapacity to think logically? A central aim of teaching, one of Piaget's disciples writes, is "to confront the child with the illogical nature of his point of view."[45] That entire, ominous-sounding approach is based on the idea that thinking, when it is logical or rational, conforms to the rules of mathematical, or propositional, logic. That claim forms the core of Piaget's educational "science." It is what underlies the recommendation of another disciple that the first two years of schooling be devoted to "exercises in manipulating, classifying, and ordering objects in ways that highlight basic operations of logical addition, multiplication, inclusion, serial ordering, and the like."[46]

But it is simply false to say that rational thought can be represented in the terms of mathematical logic. Indeed, what is most surprising about that claim is that it is presented by Piaget, and taken by his followers, as a revolutionary breakthrough in thinking about how the mind works. In fact, it is an old idea, one with which philosophers and logicians have been familiar for centuries. The 19th-century logician George Boole, for example, said that his aim was to discover the laws of thought and describe them in mathematical terms, "in the symbolic language of a Calculus."[47]

Still earlier, Leibniz had conceived of a mathematically precise language, a "Characteristica Universalis." The advantage of such a language, he thought, would be that disputes could be resolved in just the way a mathematical problem is solved, by calculating. If someone disagreed with him about any issue, Leibniz said, "I would say to him: 'Let us calculate, Sir,' and thus by taking pen and ink, we should settle the question."[48]

[45]I. E. Sigel, "The Piagetian System and the World of Education," quoted in Charles J. Brainerd, *Piaget's Theory of Intelligence* (Englewood Cliffs, N.J.: Prentice-Hall, 1978), p. 282.

[46]Bärbel Inhelder, Memorandum prepared for the National Academy of Sciences conference at Woods Hole, Massachusetts, September 1959, quoted in Jerome Bruner, *The Process of Education* (Cambridge, Mass.: Harvard University Press, 1960), p. 46.

[47]George Boole, *Laws of Thought* in *Collected Logical Works* (Chicago: Open Court, 1940), vol. 2, p. 1.

[48]Gottfried Wilhelm von Leibniz, *Selections*, ed. Philip P. Wiener (New York: Scribner, 1951), p. 18.

But, as is well known, neither Boole nor Leibniz, nor before them Plato, succeeded in producing such a calculus. The most recent effort, that of Bertrand Russell and Alfred North Whitehead in *Principia Mathematica*, despite the enormous mental power displayed, also resulted in failure.

The reason for the failure, it has become clear, is that human thought and language cannot be adequately represented by a symbol system that is mathematically precise. Such a system, though it may be quite useful for certain kinds of calculations, will necessarily leave out many nuances of meaning that exist in natural language. For example, consider the logical formula "$p \wedge q$," read as "p and q." Substituting for p the statement "It is raining" and for q the statement "It is cold," $p \wedge q$ becomes "It is raining and it is cold." It would, however, be a mistake to conclude that the logical symbol $\wedge$ is an exact equivalent of the English word "and." Indeed, if one focuses on the rules governing the use of $\wedge$, one can see quite clearly that it is not an exact equivalent. According to the rules of propositional logic, "$p \wedge q$" is equivalent to "$q \wedge p$." If it is raining and it is cold, then it is cold and it is raining. But, though the transposition does no harm here, there are many other statements the meaning of which would be changed by that operation. Thus "They got married and had a child" or "He set to work and found a job" are not at all logically equivalent to "They had a child and got married" or "He found a job and set to work."[49]

The point is that the English word "and" often has temporal connotations that the logical symbol $\wedge$ never does. Similar differences of meaning obtain with regard to the other terms of propositional logic and their English "counterparts." There is, in fact, only an inexact approximation between propositional logic and natural language. To have as a basic assumption, as Piaget's theory does, that propositional logic is identical with logical thought is to misrepresent logical thought from the outset. When that false theory is implemented, it results in the opposite of what is intended. It is intended to help children become clearer in their thinking, but it succeeds only in confusing them.

An atmosphere of patronizing authoritarianism, grounded in a simplistic view of thinking, pervades Piaget's interaction with children. It can be seen, for example, in the way he talks to children

[49]P. F. Strawson, *Introduction to Logical Theory* (London: Methuen, 1952), p. 80.

23

about their ideas concerning various features of the world, the nature of causality, the relationship between words and their meaning, the concepts of thinking and of dreaming, the nature of consciousness, the idea of the self. In each case Piaget comes to the discussion with the assumption that what the child has to say is bound to be incorrect, or illogical, since it represents a stage of mental development at which the mind is illogical. The child's thought is only a stage on the way to the correct, adult, fourth-stage view of causality or meaning.

But that is an unreasonable approach to take. After all, the issues involved are among the most complex and controversial in the whole history of human thought. Philosophers, adults all, have had not a single view but many different views on those matters. For example, materialists, idealists, epiphenomenalists, interactionists, parallelists, and others have had different ideas about the nature of consciousness. In *The Mind and Its Place in Nature*, C. D. Broad describes 11 different views on the issue.[50] How could one think, as Piaget does, that there is such a thing as the adult view of consciousness or causality or linguistic meaning? The answer would seem to be that Piaget is simply not a very self-critical thinker. What he does is adopt one of the traditional philosophical views on each of the questions he talks about with children. For example, with respect to the concept of consciousness, he embraces traditional dualism. But he doesn't examine the view. He doesn't notice that there are problems with it, just as he doesn't notice that there are problems with his conception of logic. The result is that he does not listen to children in an open-minded way. And so he fails to see the delightful and intriguing character of many of the responses he gets. Indeed, he is quite impatient with children's imaginative flights of fancy, which he calls "romancing." And he makes it clear that he will not tolerate it. "One would like to be able to rule out romancing with the same severity as [a response intended simply to please the questioner]." At this point, as the philosopher Gareth Matthews observes, "the soft outline of the friendly Swiss psychologist, puffing reflectively on his curved-stem pipe, perceptibly hardens into the stern features of the no-nonsense schoolmaster and disciplinarian."[51]

[50]C. D. Broad, *The Mind and Its Place in Nature* (London: Routledge & Kegan Paul, 1925), pp. 43–133.

[51]Gareth B. Matthews, *Philosophy and the Young Child* (Cambridge, Mass.: Harvard University Press, 1980), p. 39.

One discussion Piaget describes is with Fav, who is seven, about dreaming. Fav had a dream in which he was standing outside his bed. Piaget asks him, "Were you in the dream or was the dream in you?" The child is inclined to say both, that the dream was in him and that he was in the dream, but to Piaget that is just an error of the pre-logical mind. The correct answer, he thinks, is that the dream was in the child. Matthews comments,

> To me the most striking aspect of this exchange is Piaget's seeming insensitivity to puzzlement. How can anybody ask anybody else, adult or child, "Were you in the dream or was the dream in you?" and not succumb to some degree of puzzlement over the naturalness, given a dream with analogous content, of the answer "Both—I was in the dream and the dream was in me." Fav is puzzled. Piaget isn't. . . .
>
> Some people are immune to philosophical puzzlement. For them there is, perhaps, much to learn about the world but nothing to puzzle over. To judge from *The Child's Conception of the World*, Piaget is himself such a person. For someone like me, by contrast, someone who still finds puzzling a great many things about thinking, meaning, dreaming, life, consciousness—the topics of Piaget's book—a child's remark . . . can start a little colloquy, with the child or with oneself, in which one tries to reason one's way out of the puzzle. . . .
>
> That philosophy can begin with a child in so simple a way says something important about philosophy, and something important about children. It is something that Piaget has missed.[52]

There is an unsettling irony in this situation. A view that claims to understand how the mind works, and intends via that understanding to help children think clearly, is in fact a limited, unreflective conception of thinking that, in its application, results in confusion and disorientation.

Piaget is not the first educator whose compassionate and wise guidance has metamorphosed into intolerant misdirection. On the contrary, that sort of transformation, mediated by false, simplistic theories, appears to be a common occurrence among educators. More attention, it would seem, ought to be given to it. For it suggests that

[52]Ibid., p. 53, 54.

the psychological mutilation *Fortune* editor Charles Silberman finds in the schools is the result, not of good ideas badly applied, but of bad ideas that look good only because they are not looked at closely enough.

2. Educational Rhetoric vs. School Reality

Educators have often expressed their ideas in grandiose rhetoric that makes it difficult to focus on what they are actually claiming. Consequently, it is difficult to see how far from the truth their claims are. For example, educational rhetoric has been unrestrained in describing what the schooling process does for children: it trains them to think rationally; it provides a foundation of moral values; it transmits the "common culture"; it enables individuals to achieve their fullest potential. But is there any correlation between those claims and the reality they allegedly describe?

The views of Horace Mann are instructive in this regard. Mann was an extremely forceful orator. The rhetorical power of his descriptions of what schooling would do for children contributed greatly to the success of the campaign to establish the public school system in Massachusetts. Schooling, he proclaimed, would "awaken the faculty of thought in all the children of the Commonwealth, give them an inquiring, outlooking, forthgoing mind."[1] But was the schooling process, as he conceived of it, likely to bring about such a result?

Mann's view of how to awaken the faculty of thought in children, it turns out, was that of a typical 19th-century schoolmaster. It involved a daily routine of grammar lessons, penmanship, name and place geography, Latin, Greek, and so on—the docile memorizing and recitation already in place in the educational system of Germany. The German schools were Mann's model for dealing with children. He toured those schools and saw them as vital, energizing places in which children were receiving something of great value.

---

[1] Horace Mann, *Lectures and Annual Reports on Education,* ed. Mary Mann (Cambridge, Mass.: Published for the editor, 1867), p. 289.

But Mann was mistaken. Independence of mind and an inquiring spirit were not being fostered in the German schools. German schooling was, as is now widely recognized, the very essence of dull, stifling, mechanical routine. Those who had to sit in the German classrooms, it is safe to say, did not share Mann's high opinion of what was going on. The author Harry Graf Kessler, for example, said that schooling was rigid and oppressive, "a mechanical process of repetition and enforced memorizing."[2] And it was ineffective, even in its own terms. Political theorist Arnold Brecht wrote, "When we left school we had had for nine years a Latin lesson every day, some days even two. At the end of this time not one of us was able to converse fluently in Latin or even to read a Latin text with ease. Not to succeed in teaching someone a language in nine years of daily instruction must be difficult. For this a German *Gymnasium* was necessary."[3]

It is worth mentioning that the supposed justification for requiring children to study Latin was the same as that used by Piaget to justify his exercises, namely, that the study of Latin strengthens the mind's capacity for rational thought. Latin was held to be a logical language. Getting children to learn its structure, so it was believed, would bring logical order to the operations of their minds. But that claim (which is still being advanced by some educators) is entirely groundless. Latin is no more logical than any other language. There are exceptions to its rules, irregularities of conjugation and so on, just as there are to the rules of every natural language. Forcing the study of Latin on children is just one among many examples of how educators, guided by baseless theories of logic and rationality, have required children to engage in useless labor.

The Rhetoric

The German schools turned everything they touched into drudgery, Kessler said. One listened to lectures and memorized innumerable disconnected facts: verb conjugations, treaty provisions, the succession of kings, chemical formulas. "Of the ideal of the humane

[2]Quoted in R. H. Samuel and R. Hinton Thomas, *Education and Society in Modern Germany* (London: Routledge & Kegan Paul, 1949), p. 17.

[3]Arnold Brecht, *The Political Education of Arnold Brecht: An Autobiography, 1884–1970* (Princeton, N.J.: Princeton University Press, 1970), p. 11.

individual, bearing in his mind and heart consciousness of all mankind and its culture," Kessler wrote, "all that remained was the enormous industry necessary to absorb the immense amount of material involved. This had acquired an independent function and usurped, as it were with satanic majesty, the throne of the old ideal of humanism."[4]

Mann's rhetoric in praise of what was actually profitless drudgery set a tone that has been echoed by innumerable educators. The most pedestrian school activities are portrayed in grand terms, as though they were profoundly beneficial, with the power to transform and enlighten people and, by replacing ignorance with understanding, to serve as a defense against the collapse of civilization itself.

Ernest Boyer, president of the Carnegie Foundation for the Advancement of Teaching, says that students are "shockingly ignorant" about far too many things. In particular, they are ignorant of "the web that we call civilization and how easily it can be torn asunder."[5] That, he claims, is a dangerous situation. If we are to prevent civilization's being torn asunder, students have to be made "fully aware," Boyer says.[6] To that end, he proposes that all high school students be required to take a one-year course on Western civilization.

One might be suspicious of the claim that anyone could become "fully aware" of the web of civilization in such a short time. But "educators are eternal optimists," Boyer says, and he claims that his envisioned course would accomplish much more than one might suppose. As a result of it, the students will gain an understanding of a great many things, he says. They will come to appreciate "how ideas about democracy flourished in early Greece"; "how our own standards of beauty were shaped by the European Renaissance"; "how philosophers and revolutionaries of the Western world have influenced our traditions of government and law"; how human communities have been organized, "from tribes to city-states and ultimately to our contemporary nation-states."[7] What is more, the

---

[4]Quoted in Samuel and Thomas, p. 17
[5]Ernest L. Boyer, *High School* (New York: Harper & Row, 1983), p. 103.
[6]Ibid.
[7]Ibid., p. 102.

students in this course are going to get a sense of "personal enlighten-ment." That will come about "as they examine historical and literary works, from *The Egyptian Book of the Dead* to Plato's *Republic* to Cicero's *Orations* to Shakespeare's *King Lear*, to name a few."[8]

Is that a realistic proposal? How could so much possibly happen in a single year? Boyer doesn't say anything about that. He doesn't go into the details, though it is the details with which the students will be confronted. The idea of the Western civilization course is left at the level of rhetoric: "Great ideas will be examined. Insight, illumination, enlightenment will be the result." Lofty words are being used casually here, with little connection to reality.

Consider the claim that the students in this course are going to gain personal enlightenment through their examination of Plato's *Republic*. Boyer is certainly right in holding that the *Republic* requires examination if it is to be read with profit. It is a work in which Plato presents his theory of knowledge, of human nature, of virtue, of social and political organization, and a defense of the metaphysical foundation of his entire outlook, the Theory of Forms. Those are not ideas that yield much to skimming.

But are those ideas of Plato really going to be examined in this Western civilization course? How does Boyer imagine it? Will there be an examination of the Theory of Forms, for example? Will the class consider the philosophical problems generated by the theory? Will there be an investigation of Plato's own suspicion that the theory contained fundamental logical flaws? Will the students explore the connection between the Theory of Forms and Plato's authoritarian political philosophy? Will they be pondering, puzzling about Plato's thought?

Boyer doesn't comment on any of that. He contents himself with saying that the students are going to get personal enlightenment. But it is hard to see how the examination of Plato's *Republic* could be expected to be very deep. The students in this course are also going to be "examining" the thought of Pericles and Cicero and St. Augustine and Hobbes and Locke and Hume and Hegel. If one throws in, as Boyer does, ancient Egyptian culture and religion and *King Lear* and Renaissance art, it begins to seem unlikely that the time spent on Plato will allow for a great deal of reflection. Nor

[8]Ibid.

does it seem likely, consequently, that the students are going acquire much understanding of Plato's thought or much insight into the issues he thought about. To speak of students' gaining "a sense of personal enlightenment" is absurd.

The Reality

What will actually happen in Boyer's Western civilization course is clear. It will consist—as such courses have always consisted—of memorizing. There will be large numbers of disconnected, and therefore essentially meaningless, facts. There will be a lot of skimming of "classics of Western thought." And there will be workbooks with entries matching philosophers and their "ideas," the latter fixed in some formulated phrase—Plato: Philosopher-King; Locke: *tabula rasa*; Hegel: phenomenology of mind; and so on.

There is no value in the collecting of such phrases. To encourage it, to force children to engage in it, is to advance a false and pedestrian view of philosophical thought. Implying, as such courses do, that associating great names with great doctrines constitutes understanding is a distortion. The whole enterprise does nothing but encourage and reward superficiality.

Boyer sees how empty such courses are as they exist, not in the rhetorical fantasies of the educator, but in the real world of the classroom. He sits in on a world history class. What he sees is students going over worksheets on the Middle Ages. Then, for the next 30 minutes the teacher lectures on the reasons Constantinople was a good location for a capital, the differences between Greek Orthodoxy and Western Christianity, and the characteristics of Gothic church architecture. The students are bored. Some are passing notes; others are sleeping. "Fragments of information, unexamined and unanalyzed, are what is being transmitted here," Boyer says.[9] Nevertheless, the teacher believes that the class was successful. He has "covered the material," and there have been no disruptions.

That is what such courses are like. Despite the extravagant phrases in which educators couch their promises of benefit, the world of the classroom—which is somehow supposed to produce the benefit—remains, by and large, what it has always been: enervating, pointless tedium.

[9]Ibid.

What could be further from what is claimed for it than that world history class? Its aims are no doubt as lofty as Boyer's. The course description no doubt speaks of providing the students with an "understanding of the human heritage" or a "lifeline across the scary chasm of our contemporary situation." But in the real world, where the details are played out, what is taking place is that someone is reciting a list of structureless facts. What theory, one wonders, scientific or otherwise, says that that is likely to lead to understanding or personal enlightenment or to anything valuable?

Although Boyer sees that something is wrong, like many educators he fails to see the nature and depth of the problem. He laments that the teacher hasn't shown any "pictures or photographs to illustrate Gothic church architecture." But the problem with the class is not the absence of audiovisual aids. The problem is that the class is, in Silberman's phrase, "intellectually and esthetically barren." It will not be transformed into a path to personal enlightenment with a little tweaking here or there. It is not that close to being meaningful.

The people in this class are being forced to listen to someone who is talking without any depth of feeling or insight or enjoyment about matters in which no one, the speaker included, has any interest at all. How, but for an illusion, could this be seen as contributing to the life of the mind? Rather, it is an abuse of the mind, turning the mind into a receptacle for trivia, forcing it to engage in the collecting of unconnected, unexamined fragments of information.

One can understand why Kessler said that something "satanic" takes place in school. The situation is Orwellian in its reversal of the truth: Memorizing Is Understanding; Confining the Mind Is Liberating the Mind; Boredom Is Fascination. Flowery words are used by educators without restraint. Words like "insight," "enlightenment," "flourishing of the mind" are used to describe a reality that contradicts them completely.

And what follows the world history class? More of the same. Maybe it will have to do with *Silas Marner* or photosynthesis or Eskimo fishing techniques or the properties of a rhombus. But the atmosphere will be the same. It will be, with rare exceptions, intellectually and aesthetically barren.

Educators (and others who believe their rhetoric) seem incapable of seeing how dreadful such offerings are. They say that such classes not only yield enlightenment but even produce joy in the process.

Horace Mann thought he saw joyful children in the German schools. So liberating and joyful were those schools, he thought, that they could not but usher in an era of democratic enlightenment in Germany. "All will be well in Prussia, politically," he wrote a friend.[10] Mann was, needless to say, mistaken about what the future had in store for Germany. But, more relevant to the present discussion, he was mistaken about what was taking place in front of his eyes.

Boyer is mistaken in the same way. Like Mann, he speaks of the "joy in living" that is being cultivated in the public schools. But what in the real world of school justifies that description? Observation indicates, on the contrary, that what is taking place in the schools is a shutting down of the mind. As much as 80 percent of the time children are simply being talked at. When they do speak, it is almost always to answer a question about a specific fact. Educators say that children ought to feel engaged and enthusiastic, that they should regard the school offerings as enlightening and mentally liberating. Boyer says that students should thank their teachers.[11] Should the students thank the world history teacher?

Educational rhetoric has not changed much from the days of Horace Mann. Nor, apart from cosmetics, have the schools. That is why one can read descriptions of the schools Mann admired and see that they are no different from those of today. The Austrian writer Stefan Zweig, who attended such a school, speaks for many in his reaction to the claim that schooling cultivates joy in living:

> I can vaguely remember that when we were seven, we had to memorize a song about "joyous and blissful childhood," and sing it in chorus. The melody of that simple, artless little song is still in my ears, but even then the words passed my lips only with difficulty and made an even less convincing impression upon my heart. For, if I am to be honest, the entire period of my schooling was nothing other than a constant and wearisome boredom, accompanied year after year by an increased impatience to escape from this treadmill. I cannot recall ever having been either "joyous" or "blissful" during that monotonous, heartless, and lifeless schooling

---

[10]Quoted in Jonathan Messerli, *Horace Mann: A Biography* (New York: Alfred A. Knopf, 1972), p. 394.

[11]Boyer, p. 163.

which thoroughly spoiled the best and freest period of our existence. . . .

For us schooling was compulsion, ennui, dreariness, a place where we had to assimilate the "science of the not-worth-knowing" in exactly measured portions—scholastic or scholastically manufactured material which we felt could have no relation to reality or to our personal interests. It was a dull, pointless learning that the old pedagogy forced upon us, not for the sake of life, but for the sake of learning. And the only truly joyful moment of happiness for which I have to thank my school was the day that I was able to shut the door behind me forever. . . .

For years after, whenever I passed by the gloomy, cheerless building I felt a sense of relief that I was no longer forced to enter this prison of our youth. And when the fiftieth anniversary of this exalted institution was being celebrated and I, as an erstwhile star pupil, was asked to deliver the address of the day in the presence of the Minister and the Mayor, I politely declined. I had no reason to be thankful to this school, and every word of that sort would have been a lie.[12]

Educational rhetoric glows with promise. But the glow is too bright, blinding educators to the reality beyond their words, a reality that reveals that for many children schooling is 12 years of suffering through profitless tedium, moving from one alienating, unsatisfying, disorienting task to another, years in which they are forced to suppress their imagination, their wit, their creativity, their very selves.

[12]Stefan Zweig, *The World of Yesterday* (Lincoln: University of Nebraska Press, 1964), pp. 28, 29.

3. The Basics: Mathematics

Mathematics has become so central a part of the school curriculum that most people take the requirement that everyone study it for granted. The question of justifying that requirement is rarely raised. When it is, something like the following is usually said: "Obviously it is necessary for children to learn mathematics. It is part of preparation for living. One couldn't begin to get along in the world without mathematics. One would be virtually helpless, cheated at every turn, unable to make any decision involving quantities. It's just practical common sense—you have to be able to add up a grocery bill and balance a checkbook."

What that practical common-sense justification demonstrates more than anything is how little thought underlies the demands made on children. Let it be granted that a person who couldn't add up a grocery bill would be seriously disadvantaged in life. That doesn't justify the mathematics curriculum. The issue is the justification for *12 years* of studying mathematics. Balancing a checkbook and adding up a grocery bill are not such difficult tasks that it requires 12 years of daily math problems to master them.

Further, practical needs don't begin to account for what actually goes on in school mathematics. Over a 12-year period children are required to learn a vast number of mathematical procedures that, for most people, have no practical value at all. They have to learn how to use logarithms and the binomial theorem, how to find square roots, how to draw sine curves, and so on. The overwhelming majority of people never use any of those concepts and procedures again—for the rest of their lives. Morris Kline, professor of mathematics at New York University, says that the defense of algebra, geometry, and trigonometry on the ground that they will be useful later in life is entirely unjustified, since only professionals in mathematical fields ever use that knowledge. But that group constitutes an extremely small percentage of the high school population.[1] Fran Lebowitz, in

[1]Morris Kline, *Why Johnny Can't Add: The Failure of the New Math* (New York: Vintage Books, 1974), p. 10.

her "Tips for Teens," puts the point somewhat more succinctly: "Stand firm in your refusal to remain conscious during algebra," she writes. "In real life, I assure you, there is no such thing as algebra."[2]

Educational theorists have themselves repudiated the practical common-sense justification of the mathematics curriculum. They have rejected it not only as misguided but as crassly utilitarian. Mathematics is not taught for the practical value of the mathematical techniques, they say. The purpose is much loftier. It is nothing less than that of training the child's mind to think logically and rationally. Mathematics, they contend, is the essence of logical thought. To acquire facility in mathematics is to acquire facility in logical thinking.

For a long time that idea has played a part in views about what children should be taught. A 17th-century educator declared, for example, that "the elements of Arithmetick and Geometry [must] be by all studied, being . . . sure guides and helps to Reason."[3]

A characteristic contemporary statement of the mind-training justification appears in *The Paideia Program*, a set of curriculum recommendations advanced by a committee of educators under the leadership of Mortimer Adler, chairman of the board and editor of the *Encyclopedia Britannica*. Every child, the committee insists, should be required to study mathematics "from arithmetic to calculus and beyond."[4]

Charles Van Doren, a member of the committee, which calls itself the Paideia Group, attempts to defend that requirement. "Why should children have to study mathematics so extensively?" Van Doren asks. The reason, he says, is that mathematics provides the mind with various "nutrients," such as "order, rigor, exactness, logical development from the simple to the complex."[5] The study of geometry is particularly valuable because Euclidean geometry

---

[2]Fran Lebowitz, "Tips for Teens," in *Social Studies* (New York: Pocket Books, 1982), p. 36.

[3]William Petty, "Advice to Mr. Samuel Hartlib for the Advancement of Some Particular Parts of Learning," in *Education in the United States: A Documentary History*, ed. Sol Cohen (New York: Random House, 1974), p. 247.

[4]Charles Van Doren, "Mathematics," in *The Paideia Program*, ed. Mortimer Adler (New York: Macmillan, 1984), p. 78.

[5]Ibid., p. 71.

possesses "a profound logical rightness." It is a field, Van Doren says, from which vagueness and inexactness have been "banished."

What is perhaps most remarkable about such claims is that educators continue to advance them although they have been decisively refuted by mathematicians. Euclidean geometry does not possess a profound logical rightness. And it is not a field from which vagueness and inexactness have been banished. For many centuries the geometrical proofs of the Greek mathematician Euclid were considered logically flawless. That changed in the 19th century, however, when the standards of mathematical proof became more rigorous. It was demonstrated that there are gaps in Euclid's proofs. There are many places where the assumptions he employs are not sufficient to make his conclusions follow by logical deduction. Another failing in Euclid's system has to do with his definitions. As the logician Stephen Barker points out, some of Euclid's definitions, far from being precise, are nothing more than "vague elucidations."[6] That, Barker says, "makes the structure of the system somewhat obscure." The claim, virtually universal among educators, that a child's thought processes will take on a "profound logical rightness" as a result of studying geometry is based on a conception of geometry that has been known for more than a century to be false.

Van Doren defends the mathematics curriculum on other grounds as well. But in doing so he only compounds his errors. He says that mathematics must be studied extensively because the logical certainty of its results gives "intense pleasure" to many students.[7] The point about intense pleasure is hardly to be taken seriously, no more so than Boyer's claim concerning the joy in living cultivated in the schools. Mathematics, Kline notes, does not appeal to 98 percent of students.[8]

The point about logical certainty demonstrates nothing so much as Van Doren's own limited acquaintance with mathematical thought. Already in the 19th century the discovery of non-Euclidean geometries had begun to shatter faith in the certainty of mathematical results. In the 20th century even more serious problems have been

[6]Stephen F. Barker, "Geometry," in *The Encyclopedia of Philosophy,* ed. Paul Edwards (New York: Free Press, 1967), vol. 3, pp. 285–86.

[7]Van Doren, p. 72.

[8]Kline, *Why Johnny Can't Add,* p. 149.

discovered in the form of contradictions in the foundations of mathematics. The resulting pessimism concerning mathematical certainty is described by Bertrand Russell:

> I wanted certainty in the kind of way in which people want religious faith. I thought that certainty is more likely to be found in mathematics than elsewhere. But I discovered that many mathematical demonstrations, which my teachers expected me to accept, were full of fallacies, and that, if certainty were indeed discoverable in mathematics, it would be in a new field of mathematics, with more solid foundations than those that had been hitherto thought secure. But as the work proceeded, I was continually reminded of the fable about the elephant and the tortoise. Having constructed an elephant upon which the mathematical world would rest, I found the elephant tottering, and proceeded to construct a tortoise to keep the elephant from falling. But the tortoise was no more secure than the elephant, and after some twenty years of very arduous toil, I came to the conclusion that there was nothing more that I could do in the way of making mathematical knowledge indubitable. . . . The splendid certainty which I had always hoped to find in mathematics was lost in a bewildering maze.[9]

There are, on today's scene, numerous opposing schools of mathematical thought, with sharp disagreement among them concerning the most fundamental questions—for example, what axioms are acceptable and even what constitutes a mathematical proof. "It is now apparent," Kline writes, "that the concept of a universally accepted, infallible body of reasoning—the majestic mathematics of 1800 and the pride of man—is a grand illusion."[10]

None of that appears in Van Doren's superficial treatment. Like many educators, he has embraced, without examination, a false, simplistic conception of mathematics. And on that basis he issues pronouncements about how mathematical thought nourishes the mind.

That superficial view of mathematics is connected with an equally superficial view of thinking. Van Doren says that children have to

---

[9]Quoted in Morris Kline, *Mathematics: The Loss of Certainty* (Oxford: Oxford University Press, 1980), pp. 229–30.

[10]Ibid., p. 6.

be trained to think rationally. They must be taught, he says, to begin with simple elements, understand those and then move on in an orderly, rule-governed way to form more complex thought structures. The trouble is that that is not an accurate representation of what thinking is or of what it ought to be. It is certainly not the way children think and learn. John Holt points out that a child "does not take one thing at a time and get it down pat before going on to the next. Instead he tries a great many different things, and gradually gets better at all of them. In learning to talk . . . he does not learn to pronounce one word perfectly before trying another. He says many words, all of them badly, and by practice gradually improves them all."[11]

That is true not only of the thought processes of the child. The greatest discoveries of the human mind have not been the result of "orderly" thinking. If anything, genuine creative thought resembles play far more than it does the rule-governed constructions of school mathematics. Einstein said that "the words of the language, as they are written or spoken, do not seem to play any role in my . . . thought." The elements of his thinking, he said, were "more or less clear images which can be 'voluntarily' reproduced and combined."[12] Such combinatory play seems to be the essential feature of productive thought—long before there is any attempt at an orderly arrangement that can be put into words. The "orderly" conception of thinking that dominates educational theorizing is a distortion that is imposed on the facts—and then on children.

The same ideas, in one form or another, make their appearance whenever educators defend the mathematics curriculum. Ernest Boyer, president of the Carnegie Foundation for the Advancement of Teaching, for example, says that children should be required to study mathematics for 12 years, not primarily to learn mathematics but to gain an understanding of "the problem-solving process."[13] There is, however, no such thing as the problem-solving process. There is no single method of solving problems, valid independent of the nature of the problem. Different sorts of problems demand

[11]Quoted in Eda J. LeShan, *The Conspiracy against Childhood* (New York: Atheneum, 1980), p. 60.

[12]Albert Einstein, *Ideas and Opinions* (New York: Bonanza Books, 1954), pp. 25–26.

[13]Ernest L. Boyer, *High School* (New York: Harper & Row, 1983), p. 108.

different methods of solution. What is more, the method of problem solving Boyer thinks children should be required to learn, that of mathematical deduction, is completely irrelevant to virtually every problem one encounters in life. Life's problems, small and large, Kline notes, "cannot be solved deductively. There are no self-evident axioms from which one can deduce what career to follow, whom to marry, or even whether to go to the movies."[14]

It is not a small matter to be training children's minds according to a view of the mind that is false. On the contrary, the mistaken conception of mathematics and its relation to thinking results in a great deal of harm to children. For what actually takes place in mathematics classes has nothing to do with thinking in any creative sense at all. It consists almost entirely of memorizing formulas and carrying out purely mechanical operations. In algebra, for example, children are taught dozens of mathematical techniques: factoring, solving equations with one and two unknowns, the multiplication and division of polynomials, and operations with negative numbers and with square roots. They are confronted with a bewildering assortment of processes that they repeat by rote. The learning, Kline writes, "is almost always sheer memorization."[15] The thinking involved in studying mathematics is, for most children, docile, uninspiring, and profitless. It consists of laboriously acquiring techniques that are then completely forgotten, never having been put to any real use.

Educators, however, their rhetoric far removed from reality, say that in studying mathematics, children's minds, in Van Doren's words, "enlarge and experience a higher degree of freedom."[16] Just as the memorizing of unconnected facts is declared to constitute a path to understanding and enlightenment, so the mastering of unconnected, mechanical operations is declared to be the path to rationality and thinking power. Once again the truth is being turned upside down. The idea that 12 years of doing mathematics problems trains the mind to think rationally should be abandoned once and for all. It is an idea whose time has gone.

---

[14]Kline, *Why Johnny Can't Add*, p. 60.
[15]Ibid., p. 7.
[16]Van Doren, p. 71.

That is not to say that mathematics is unimportant. Of course it is important. But that doesn't mean that it is the foundation of all logical thought, or even that it is the preferred way of thinking about things. To treat it as such is to impose a false standard on children. Mathematics represents one kind, or perhaps several kinds, of thinking. But not all rational or fruitful or perceptive thought is of those kinds. As many philosophers have pointed out, there are aspects of reality that get distorted when one imposes a mathematical model on them. One of the greatest mathematicians, Pascal, describing the difference between the "mathematical mind" and the "perceptive mind," put it this way:

> The reason that mathematicians are not perceptive is that they do not see what is in front of them, and that, accustomed to the exact and plain principles of mathematics, and not reasoning till they have well inspected and arranged their principles, they are lost in matters of perception where the principles do not allow for such arrangement. . . . Mathematicians wish to treat matters of perception mathematically, and make themselves ridiculous.[17]

That idea was advanced even more forcefully by the Italian philosopher Giambattista Vico, who made it a cornerstone of his thought. Vico criticized, as a fundamental mistake, Descartes's claim that the methods of geometry, of mathematical deduction, are applicable everywhere. He argued that those methods produce distorted thinking when they are used in areas where they don't belong, such as poetry and rhetoric. Vico rejected, as a form of "pedagogic despotism," the idea that the deductive method is the sole or preferred path to knowledge.[18] It is an approach, he said, that suppresses other aspects of mental development, especially those involving the imagination.

Some people think well mathematically. But many others do not. They are sensitive to different aspects of reality—its aesthetic properties, or its ethical dimensions. For such people mathematical thinking is limiting, stifling, and has little to do with what they want to know. The attempt to force them to think mathematically is a mistake of

[17]Blaise Pascal, *Pensées* (New York: E. P. Dutton, 1958), p. 1.

[18]Isaiah Berlin, "Vico's Concept of Knowledge," in *Against the Current* (Harmondsworth, U.K.: Penguin Books, 1979), p. 112.

the same kind as, but far more serious than, the attempt to force a child to be right-handed. It is far more serious because it exacts a much greater psychological toll.

Educators claim that they are using the mathematics curriculum to train children to think logically. In reality they are squandering children's resources, confusing and frightening them, shattering their confidence and self-esteem. Because the mastery of an arbitrary grab bag of mathematical techniques is thought to be of great value, the damage is ignored. Or if it is noticed, it is seen as a necessary evil, the price people have to pay for learning how to think rationally. But it is an entirely unnecessary evil. The case in favor of the 12-year mathematics curriculum is wrong about the nature of mathematics, wrong about the nature of thinking, and wrong about the relation between the two.

4. The Basics: Reading

One might think that the case for traditional schooling is strongest with respect to reading. Reading, after all, is a part of most lives in a way in which logarithms and the binomial theorem are not. The approach to reading that one finds in the schools, however, exhibits the same mistakes that are made in connection with mathematics, along with some new ones. The result is that instead of helping children to read and to enjoy reading, schooling causes many children to experience reading as entirely unconnected with pleasure. Moreover, the techniques employed in teaching reading are themselves among the principal causes of reading difficulties and much needless psychological distress.

The fundamental mistake is to regard reading ability, like mathematical ability, as a reliable measure of intelligence, of general mental functioning. That erroneous idea has led to enormous pressure on children, by teachers and some parents, to read as early as possible, as much as possible, and even as fast as possible. Getting a child to read early, the belief is, accelerates the development of the child's intelligence and enables it to reach levels it would not otherwise reach.

That is a seductive idea, easy to believe, as is shown by the growing number of programs, both inside and outside the schools, promising to develop "superkids." Numerous books and articles have appeared explaining how to give your child a superior mind, teach your baby to read, and train your baby to be a genius. But the premise is false. Those who have looked at the facts, as opposed to the rhetoric, know that it is false. David Elkind, professor of child study at Tufts University, writes, "There is absolutely no evidence that such teaching . . . has any effect on a child's brightness."[1] In an exhaustive study of the available data, Raymond and Dorothy Moore conclude, "No long-term advantage results from rushing the child in

---

[1] David Elkind, *Miseducation* (New York: Alfred A. Knopf, 1987), p. 13.

reading."[2] Not only are those pressures unhelpful, they are harmful. "Pressuring children to read at a level for which they are not prepared, including pressures to keep up with peers in the classroom, results in frustration, reading rebellion, and ... many cases of so-called reading disability."[3] The damage caused has become so apparent that it is even beginning to be recognized, though not nearly widely enough, within the educational establishment itself. Helen Hefferman, chief of elementary education in the California State Department of Education, says that "a mountain of evidence" shows that the attempt to force a child to read before he is ready "may result in some evidence of reading, but at an excessive cost in physiological and psychological damage and at great risk of impairing his interest in reading."[4]

Reading and Understanding

If one looks at how pressure to read is applied, it is not difficult to understand what produces the damage. *Reading Instruction for Today's Children* by Nila Banton Smith, professor of education at New York University, is a textbook for teachers of reading offering "practical suggestions ... teachers may draw upon in implementing their skill-development programs."[5] As Smith sees it, more attention must be devoted to "reading improvement in general, including a special consideration of rate in reading as a very important skill area to be cultivated."[6] To improve reading speed, the teacher is instructed, as a first step, to test the children to see how fast they do read:

> Prepare for this test by making up ten questions on the content of three or four pages of a story in a basic reader which [the children] have not read.
> Have the children find the page on which the story begins, keeping a finger in the place and immediately closing the

---

[2]Raymond S. Moore and Dorothy N. Moore, *School Can Wait* (Provo, Utah: Brigham Young University Press, 1979), p. 108.

[3]Ibid.

[4]Quoted in Eda J. LeShan, *The Conspiracy against Childhood* (New York: Atheneum, 1980), p. 108.

[5]Nila Banton Smith, *Reading Instruction for Today's Children* (Englewood Cliffs, N.J.: Prentice-Hall, 1963), p. vi.

[6]Ibid., p. 354.

book. Provide yourself with a stop-watch if one is available; if not, use an ordinary watch with a second hand. When the second hand is at 12:00 or 6:00 (for convenience in time-keeping) give the children the signal to start reading. Allow them to read silently for three minutes, then give them the signal to stop. Each child may make a faint lead-pencil dot (which later can be erased) at the point he has reached when the "stop" signal was given.

Place on the chalkboard the ten questions which you had prepared. Ask the children to write the answers to the questions with their books closed.

After the answers are written each pupil checks his own paper as you give the answers orally. A score of ten should be allowed for each correct answer.

Following the checking of the answers, ask each pupil to count the number of words he read and divide the number by three. This will indicate the number of words per minute that he read. Have this number written on the answer paper along with the score on questions relating to the content.

Gather up the papers and without giving the names of the pupils write the rate scores on the board, ranging from the highest to the lowest, with the question score to the right of the rate score in each case.

Use the scores as the basis for discussion. Point out the variation in both speed and grasp of content. Call attention particularly to the relationship between speed and grasp of content. Some scores will show that pupils read very fast and still answer all the questions correctly. This should be held up as a desired standard, but one that can still be improved in speed. . . .

Following the discussion return the papers so that each child may place himself in the total distribution.[7]

Is it any wonder that such a practice makes reading unpleasant? The child is required to read something in which he or she has no interest, to read it as quickly as possible, and then to answer questions constructed by someone who also has no interest in what was read. That is just one example of how lifeless identification quizzes arise, with questions such as Who had the lean and hungry look? Whose cousin was Alicia? Who delivered the coffee on Wednesday? Apart from the frenzy and anxiety produced, the entire approach

[7]Ibid., p. 368.

is dominated by a false conception of what it means to understand what one reads. Understanding, in this framework, is equated with the ability to answer factual questions. But that is a shallow conception of understanding. There are innumerable ways to read and profit from what one reads. It is important to recognize that different people do it differently.

The Nobel laureate economist and social philosopher Friedrich Hayek writes,

> What . . . does my knowledge consist of on which I base my claim to be a trained economist? Certainly not in the distinct recollection of particular statements or arguments. I generally will not be able to reproduce the contents of a book I have read or a lecture I have heard on my subject. But I have certainly often greatly profited from such books or lectures, of the contents of which I could not possibly give an account even immediately after I had read or heard them. In fact the attempt to remember what the writer or speaker said would have deprived me of most of the benefit of the exposition. . . . Even as a student I soon gave up all attempts to take notes of lectures—as soon as I tried I ceased to understand. My gain from hearing or reading what other people thought was that it changed, as it were, the colors of my own concepts. What I heard or read did not enable me to reproduce their thought but altered my thought. I would not retain their ideas or concepts but modify the relations between my own.[8]

The 18th-century German thinker Georg Christoph Lichtenberg said, in a similar vein, "I forget most of what I read, just as I forget most of what I eat; but I know that both contribute, nevertheless, to the nourishment of my mind and my body."[9]

Dominated by a simplistic, fact-oriented view of understanding, Smith's approach to reading deprives it of meaning. It is reading with all the sap and juice removed.

Smith goes on to offer advice for dealing with those children whom the test shows to be slow readers. Some may not be reading

---

[8]F. A. Hayek, "Two Types of Mind," in *New Studies in Philosophy, Politics, Economics and the History of Ideas* (London: Routledge & Kegan Paul, 1978), p. 52.

[9]Georg Christoph Lichtenberg, "Aphorismen," in *Werke in Einem Band* (Hamburg: Hoffmann und Campe, 1967), p. 23 (author's translation).

fast enough, she says, because they are moving their lips. That must be corrected. Under the heading, "Breaking Habits of Bodily Movements," she writes, "Lip-reading . . . normally disappears at second grade level. If it persists at this time, concentrated attention should be directed toward breaking the habit."[10] There follows a set of instructions on how to do that.

> 1. Make children themselves conscious of the desirability of eliminating lip movement as a means of helping them to become better readers.
> 2. Watch the children during study periods and frequently remind the lip-reader to "read with your eyes."
> 3. Place printed slogans around the room, such as "Fast readers use their eyes not their lips," "Eyes are for reading; lips are for talking."
> 4. Have the persistent lip-readers place a finger or a pencil over their lips while reading. Instruct them to press down on the lips when they feel them moving and hold them still.
> 5. For variety have the lip-readers hold a piece of paper between the lips while reading. When lip-reading begins the paper drops and the pupil becomes conscious that he is moving his lips.[11]

How involving can reading be when one is so monitored and restricted? How enjoyable can it be with a piece of paper in one's mouth?

The school system creates meaningless races to promote the goal of reading faster or reading "at grade level." Not only do those races take the pleasure out of reading, but, in addition, they constitute an assault on individuality. The atmosphere produced by all the pushing and monitoring, Eda LeShan writes, reflects an "hysterical and ill-conceived impatience with growth and [an] intolerance of the normal, gradual, individual ways in which children grow."[12] LeShan describes how a first-grade teacher boasted of having gotten 90 percent of her students to read at the fifth-grade level. The principal was so impressed that he had the teacher give a seminar for the other first-grade teachers. A few months later, however, the training program had to be abandoned because parents were reporting that

[10]Smith, p. 365.
[11]Ibid.
[12]LeShan, p. 150.

their six-year-old children were unable to sleep or had headaches, stomach aches, and crying spells.

Educators, in their endeavors to improve mental abilities, have become desensitized. They do not see how inhumanely they are treating children. They think that their approach to reading, based on "pedagogical science," is helping children. But it is neither scientific nor helpful. And it is certainly not an approach that encourages reading for pleasure. H. L. Mencken saw it coming:

> The old pedagogy has gone out, and a new and complicated science has taken its place. Unluckily, it is largely the confection of imbeciles, and so the unhappiness of the young continues. In the whole realm of human learning there is no faculty more fantastically incompetent than that of pedagogy. If you doubt it, go read the pedagogical journals.
>
> The school-children of today are exposed to this cataract of puerility from the time they escape from the kindergarten until the time they escape into college or wage-slavery.[13]

Prescribed Reading

The harm done by the "scientific" teaching of reading is only part of the story. There is another aspect of the traditional school approach to reading that is even more harmful and constitutes even more of an assault on individuality. Educators want to determine not only when children should read and how they should read but also what they should read. The idea is to use reading, as mathematics is used, to "nourish the mind." But their judgments about the mental nourishment provided by literature are no more to be trusted than their judgments about the mental nourishment provided by algebra. For one thing—apart from their foisting a superficial, fact-oriented conception of reading on children—there is the record of their selections. They are, after all, the ones who have bored millions with their choices of reading material, from the bloodless textbooks one must read by the dozens to *Silas Marner*.

Should there be a group of people deciding what everyone reads? Are there experts who are in a position to answer the question, What should a person read? I think not. Educators claim expertise, but their attempts to justify that claim are less than persuasive.

---

[13]H. L. Mencken, "Travail," in *A Mencken Chrestomathy* (New York: Alfred A. Knopf, 1949), p. 310.

Diane Ravitch and Chester Finn are two educators who claim to know, not only what every child should be reading, but also what proportion of a child's reading should be in each of various literary genres. According to them, the reading should be distributed as follows:

Novels, short stories, and plays: 50 percent
Myths, epics, biblical characters and stories: 30 percent
Poetry: 10 percent
Nonfiction: 10 percent

That list is already grounds for suspicion. What is the justification for the assignment of percentages? Surprisingly, Ravitch and Finn do not even attempt to provide one. They say simply that they were on an educational committee and that "the committee decided to distribute emphasis to the different genres in the [above] manner."[14] But why the committee made that decision is not explained. And what reason could there be? The committee's determination would seem to be completely arbitrary. Indeed, many of the claims Ravitch and Finn make seem to be based on nothing but arbitrary decisions.

As part of a group calling itself the Educational Excellence Network, Ravitch and Finn administered nationwide a test on history and literature to 17-year-olds. The results demonstrate, they say, that children are not reading enough works in the various literature categories. That must be changed. The schools must require that they read more.

But which works should they be required to read? Ravitch and Finn say that making selections is a "critical problem" in devising a curriculum. The difficulty of the problem becomes apparent when one considers the large number of authors described by Ravitch and Finn as "major." The selections must be made from among Shakespeare, Dickens, Wordsworth, Keats, Twain, Whitman, Blake, Dickinson, Hawthorne, the Brontës, Chaucer, Dostoevsky, Emerson, Frost, Melville, Poe, Hemingway, Ibsen, Lincoln, Sophocles, Thoreau, Tolstoy, Baldwin, London, Donne, Fitzgerald, Kafka, Orwell, Plato, Stowe, Swift, Tennyson, Wright, Yeats, Austen, Byron, Coleridge, Eliot, Faulkner, Franklin, Shelley, Hardy, Carroll, Woolf,

[14]Diane Ravitch and Chester Finn, *What Do Our 17-Year-Olds Know?* (New York: Harper and Row, 1987), p. 40.

Welty, Steinbeck, Bellow, Sandburg, Alcott, Hansberry, Doyle, Williams, Miller, Irving, Cooper, Solzhenitsyn, Cummings, O'Neill, Lawrence, de Tocqueville, King, Jefferson, Douglass, Machiavelli, Dubois, Mill, and Darwin. That, as Ravitch and Finn rightly say, is "a massive menu of literary greats."[15]

Ravitch and Finn are aware that educators have not been able to agree on which writers children should read. There has been no uniform answer to the critical problem because there is no generally agreed-upon standard. That results in a situation in which subjective, arbitrary answers have been given by educators. And the answers have been widely disparate.

Ravitch and Finn find that situation unfortunate. "Something of value is lost," they say, "when there is no . . . professional consensus about which writers and which works are superior."[16] But how can one arrive at a professional consensus without a standard? Fortunately, according to Ravitch and Finn, there is a standard. One should adopt, they contend, "a standard of the *best* literature for all youngsters: the best novels, the best short stories, the best poems, the best plays, the best essays."[17]

That standard hardly provides a solution to the "critical problem." Educators who disagree about which books children should read are not likely to agree about which books are the best. Ravitch and Finn have not solved the problem. They have simply re-raised it in a slightly different form. In no place do they give a justification for selecting some authors and excluding others. Nowhere do they give any criteria for answering the question, Which are the best? The answer to that question, for all that they say, would seem to be no less subjective and arbitrary than the answer to the question, What percentage of a child's reading should be devoted to the various genres?

But even if it turned out that every educator agreed with Ravitch and Finn about which are "the best," why should everyone have to read the works so designated? Suppose Ravitch and Finn were to announce that "Dostoevsky is one of the best for sure, but Jack London doesn't quite make it." And suppose further that every school principal or school board agreed with them. Why should everyone have to read Dostoevsky? What if Dostoevsky's writing doesn't touch

[15]Ibid.
[16]Ibid.
[17]Ibid, p. 210. Italics in the original.

somebody, isn't found to be relevant to that person's concerns? That can't happen, according to Ravitch and Finn. "The best literature," they say, "has the power to touch the lives of whoever reads it, to make them understand themselves better because of what they have read, to make them sensitive to the joys and sufferings of others, to awaken them to knowledge and emotions that are both particular and universal."[18] That is why, presumably, educators don't have to take individual reactions into account. If they have succeeded in picking out "the best," then it will be relevant to everybody.

What Ravitch and Finn say about the best literature, however, is not an accurate description of reality but only empty rhetoric. The best literature, by whatever standard, does not touch everybody who reads it. There isn't a single work ever written that has the power to touch everybody. People are too different. There is no writer who hasn't been found boring or superficial or irrelevant by some people. Ralph Waldo Emerson, who is on most educational lists, including that of Ravitch and Finn, doesn't appeal to everyone. The English poet Swinburne didn't think that Emerson helped him understand himself better. Emerson, he said, was "a gap-toothed and hoary-headed ape, carried at first into notice on the shoulders of Carlyle, and who now in his dotage spits and chatters from a dirtier perch of his own finding and fouling."[19] Nietzsche expressed his distaste in a somewhat milder fashion: "Emerson is one who lives instinctively on ambrosia—and leaves everything indigestible on his plate."[20] Emerson, for his part, was not a great admirer of Charles Dickens: "He is a painter of English details . . . ; local and temporary in his tints and style, and local in his aims."[21] George Meredith went further: "Dickens was the incarnation of cockneydom, a caricaturist who aped the moralist; he should have kept to short stories. If his novels are read at all in the future people will wonder what we saw in him."[22] Thoreau is another favorite of educators.

[18]Ibid., p. 221.

[19]Cecil Y. Lang, ed., *The Swinburne Letters* (New Haven, Conn.: Yale University Press, 1959), vol. 2, p. 274.

[20]Friedrich Nietzsche, *Twilight of the Idols*, in *The Portable Nietzsche*, ed. Walter Kaufmann (New York: Viking, 1954), p. 522.

[21]Ralph Waldo Emerson, *English Traits* (New York: P. F. Collier & Son, 1909), p. 439.

[22]George Meredith, *Letters: Collected and Edited by His Son* (New York: Charles Scribner's Sons, 1912), vol. 2, p. 603.

But he also didn't appeal to everyone. Robert Louis Stevenson said of him, "Thoreau's thin, penetrating, big-nosed face, even in a bad woodcut, conveys some hint of the limitations of his mind and character. With his almost acid sharpness of insight, with his almost animal dexterity in act, there went none of that large, unconscious geniality of the world's heroes. He was not easy, not ample, not urbane, not even kind."[23] Is Shakespeare an exception? No. Tolstoy, not an insensitive man, wrote, "The works of Shakespeare, borrowed as they are, and externally, like mosaics, artificially fitted together piecemeal from bits invented for the occasion, have nothing whatever in common with art and poetry."[24] George Bernard Shaw put his reaction to Shakespeare in somewhat more extreme terms: "With the single exception of Homer, there is no eminent writer, not even Sir Walter Scott, whom I can despise so entirely as I despise Shakespeare. . . . It would positively be a relief to me to dig him up and throw stones at him."[25]

The claim that great literature speaks to everyone is a characteristic example of educational rhetoric. However, that claim is not examined, and so the fact that it bears no relation to the real world passes unnoticed. Greatness is no more universally appealing in literature than it is in any other area of human endeavor. No more than in music, for example. Mozart is presumably a musical great if anyone is. But that does not mean that his music speaks to everyone. The pianist Glenn Gould found Mozart's music "intolerable, loaded with quasi-theatrical conceit, . . . an appalling collection of clichés."[26] To Tchaikovsky's ears and soul, Brahms was a "self-conscious mediocrity."[27] For Nietzsche, Bach's music was marred by "too much crude Christianity, crude Germanism, crude scholasticism."[28]

---

[23]Robert Louis Stevenson, "Henry David Thoreau: His Character and Opinions," in *Familiar Studies of Men and Books* (New York: Charles Scribner's Sons, 1907), p. 116.

[24]Leo Tolstoy, "Shakespeare and the Drama," in *Recollections and Essays* (New York: Oxford University Press, 1937), p. 339.

[25]George Bernard Shaw, "Blaming the Bard," in *Shaw on Shakespeare*, ed. Edwin Wilson (New York: E. P. Dutton, 1961), p. 54.

[26]Otto Friedrich, *Glenn Gould* (New York: Vintage Books, 1989), pp. 143, 145.

[27]Modeste Tchaikovsky, *The Life and Letters of Peter Ilich Tchaikovsky* (New York: Haskell House, 1970), p. 519.

[28]Friedrich Nietzsche, *Human, All-Too-Human* (New York: Russell & Russell, 1964), part 2, p. 267.

Ravitch and Finn have a simplistic view of greatness, just as Smith had a simplistic view of understanding. If the power to speak to everyone were a test of greatness, nothing ever produced could be called great. There is no single test of greatness, but what is often true is that great works come from the heart and they come with power. It is, however, the power of an individual, and it will not be suited to every other individual.

Ravitch and Finn make other, equally unexamined, claims about reading. Their test reveals that "our society is breeding a new strain of cultural barbarian," people who are able to communicate only at the most rudimentary level.[29] The reason they are not able to communicate better is that they don't read enough and so don't know enough about history and literature. A central task of schooling is to improve their powers of communication.

Reading and Communication

What Ravitch and Finn say about communication is as one-dimensional as what they say about greatness: "To the extent that we are knowledgeable about [history and literature], we are better able to communicate with one another. And the more knowledgeable we are, the more complicated are the discussions that we can have together."[30] That is not an insightful analysis of communication. There is no such simple formula characterizing the relationship between knowledge of history and literature and the ability to communicate. Are the best communicators the most knowledgeable people? Are professors of history and literature the best communicators? Perhaps Ravitch and Finn have never encountered a learned pedant. Or perhaps they have forgotten Pope's description of the "bookful blockhead ignorantly read, with loads of learned lumber in his head."[31]

What is involved in human communication in the real world is far more subtle than what emerges from their account. Think of some of the factors that are involved in being a good communicator: vulnerability, listening well, caring, wit. Factual knowledge may be

[29]Ravitch and Finn, p. 13.

[30]Ibid., p. 251.

[31]Alexander Pope, *An Essay on Criticism*, ed. E. Audra and Aubrey Williams (London: Methuen, 1961), p. 309.

on the list, but it is certainly not the only item. Nor is it even near the top. There is no one key to communication, but if something did have to be mentioned, it would be, not knowledge, but personality. And that is exactly what the notion of a reading list valid for everyone—a literature canon—ignores altogether.

Improving the ability of people to communicate is a frequent theme of educators. E. D. Hirsch Jr., another member of the Educational Excellence Network, shares with Ravitch and Finn the view that children should be required to read more of "the best" literature so that their powers of communication will be enhanced. He gives the following illustration of how familiarity with Shakespeare can help one communicate.

> My father used to write business letters that alluded to Shakespeare. These allusions were effective for conveying complex messages to his associates. . . . For instance, in my father's commodity business, the timing of sales and purchases was all-important, and he would sometimes write or say to his colleagues, "There is a tide," without further elaboration. Those four words carried not only a lot of complex information, but also the persuasive force of a proverb. In addition to the basic practical meaning, "Act now!" what came across was a lot of implicit reasons why immediate action was important.[32]

Hirsch quotes the passage in *Julius Caesar* from which the words are taken:

> There is a tide in the affairs of men
> Which taken at the flood leads on to fortune;
> Omitted, all the voyage of their life
> Is bound in shallows and miseries.
> On such a full sea are we now afloat,
> And we must take the current when it serves,
> Or lose our ventures.

He comments:

> To say "There is a tide" is better than saying "Buy (or sell) now and you'll cover expenses for the whole year, but

---

[32]E. D. Hirsch Jr., *Cultural Literacy: What Every American Needs to Know* (Boston: Houghton Mifflin, 1987), p. 9.

54

if you fail to act right away, you may regret it the rest of your life." That would be twenty-seven words instead of four, and while the bare message of the longer statement would be conveyed, the persuasive force wouldn't. Think of the demands of such a business communication. To persuade somebody that your recommendation is wise and well-founded, you have to give lots of reasons and cite known examples and authorities. My father accomplished that and more in four words, which made quoting Shakespeare as effective as any efficiency consultant could wish.[33]

There are many claims in this passage that are not true. As an account of the demands of business communication, it is certainly not generally applicable. To say that a business recommendation must cite authorities in order to be well-founded is to offer a careless and false generalization. Are authorities cited in every persuasive business communication? And must there always be lots of reasons? Isn't one sometimes enough? Imagine receiving the note, "Buy Martex. The price is going to double overnight." If the note came from your millionaire acquaintance, Stanley the stock market whiz, would you insist on lots more reasons? And what does it mean to say that a persuasive business communication must cite known examples? Known examples of what? Buying? Selling?

The main point, though, is that Hirsch's claim about what his father accomplished is false. He says that by quoting Shakespeare his father gave lots of reasons for accepting his business recommendation. How does quoting Shakespeare show that his recommendation is well-founded? Clearly it doesn't. Didn't Mr. Hirsch Sr. ever make an ill-founded recommendation and "support" it with that same quote? Were his readings of the tide always right? And even if he never made a mistake, the Shakespeare quote is irrelevant to the question of whether or not his recommendation is well-founded. The quote not only fails to show that Hirsch Sr.'s business recommendation is well-founded; it does not provide the slightest reason for believing it to be so. It doesn't tell one whether to buy or sell, and it doesn't give a reason for doing either.

The persuasiveness doesn't reside in the quote. Since Hirsch's father had a substantial record of success, it is not surprising that

[33]Ibid.

his recommendations were found to be persuasive. If he had had a record of failure, all the Shakespeare in the world wouldn't have helped.

Such analyses of communication fall far short of justifying the demands of Ravitch, Finn, and Hirsch that children be required to read the literature they have designated as "the best." But the demands do not stop there. Educators insist on determining not only what books are worth reading but what facts are worth knowing.

Ravitch and Finn tested children on a wide variety of topics. And in every case the children came up short. The vast majority did not know what Ravitch and Finn determined to be worth knowing. Their performance is said to have been "shameful" when they were asked about such matters as the American role in Korea; Sputnik; Betty Friedan and Gloria Steinem; "nullification"; the exploration of the Missouri Valley; "how the presence of isolating geographic factors, like a mountain range or a desert, affects cultural development; and how physical characteristics of the land affect migration patterns, trade routes, invasions, wars, and economic development."[34] The children were unfamiliar with the history of the trade union movement. They didn't know who wrote *The Minister's Black Veil, Young Goodman Brown,* and *Rappaccini's Daughter* (Nathaniel Hawthorne). They were ignorant not only of *Antigone* but also of *Paradise Lost.* They couldn't say which colony was founded by John Winthrop and the Puritans (Boston, not Plymouth as most of the test takers thought).

But is the justification for demanding knowledge of those matters any firmer than the justification for demanding that children read the books Ravitch and Finn select? What Ravitch and Finn offer in the way of justification turns out to be another pseudostandard, like "the best," a standard that allows them to demand whatever they want—to impose their subjective values in the guise of something objectively established.

Why, for example, should it be demanded of children that they read about the history of the trade union movement? It is necessary, Ravitch and Finn say, because "the labor movement story is one of men and women, laws and campaigns, ideas and conflict. This is

[34]Ravitch and Finn, pp. 201, 210.

56

the stuff of history."[35] Like "the best," that is no standard at all. To what wouldn't it apply? How does it pick out the story of the labor union movement and not the story of abstract expressionism or the Battle of Britain or empiricism or major league baseball? Everything in history is the stuff of history. Why is it important to focus on the struggles of Samuel Gompers and not those of Bach or Claus von Stauffenberg or Jackie Robinson or Sophie Scholl?

Why just Ravitch and Finn's selections? Why their slice of the human experience? They say that those are the things one must know if one is going to be able "to understand what others are debating."[36] But, in the first place, it is unclear why the focus of one's interests should be determined by what others are debating. In the second place, that is another pseudocriterion. Others are debating a million things: abortion, the rights of defendants, the name of the new stadium, the future of Eastern Europe, the relationship between free will and determinism, the new French cinema. So the question remains, Why should one know about the matters that Ravitch and Finn pick out? The only answer would seem to be that those are the things that interest Ravitch and Finn.

They contend that "these are the kinds of specifics it is necessary to know in order to understand how the society we inhabit came to be as it is."[37] But there are many different ways of understanding how the society we inhabit came to be as it is. There is no more a specific set of facts required for understanding a society than there is a specific set of facts required for understanding a book, or a person. Ravitch and Finn's view about what one needs in order to understand is as unfounded as their view about what one needs in order to communicate.

That kind of fact-oriented insensitivity to what is organic and alive is not a new phenomenon among educators. On the contrary, it has long been characteristic of their mentality and their approach to children. In his capacity as secretary of the Board of Education of Massachusetts, Horace Mann prepared a list of books he considered suitable for school libraries. He wanted to include *Two Years before the Mast* by Richard Henry Dana Jr., but he found it unacceptable

[35]Ibid., p. 68.
[36]Ibid.
[37]Ibid.

as written. So he made a personal visit to Dana to discuss the problem. Mann said that the book could be included if Dana were willing to make some "slight modifications." Mann wanted more facts. Dana should add to the novel, Mann said, "as much of exact information as possible, in regard to the geography, natural features of the countries visited, the customs, manners, etc. etc. of the people seen, together with some of the natural productions—botanical and zoological—of different places." Understandably, Dana was "astounded by Mann's presumption." He

> politely explained that "there was such a thing as unity in a book," and that to take his narrative and burden it with statistics and didactics "would destroy its character, almost as it would that of a drama." Mann responded by insisting that "a narrative, a description, had no value except as it conveyed some moral lesson or some useful fact." Since Dana's book was an interesting narrative, Mann thought it "should be made use of for valuable purposes. . . ." Only gradually realizing what had taken place in his office after Mann had left, Dana concluded that he had never seen "such an exhibition of gaucheness and want of tact" in his life. "If some enemy," he later wrote, "had employed him to come to try my patience to the utmost, he could not have executed his task better." Before him had been nothing less than the manifestation of "a school-master gone crazy."[38]

Mann's recommendation was overbearing and presumptuous. His greatest presumption, though, was his belief that he was the authority on what makes something valuable. That presumption of the educator is especially evident with regard to reading. An oft-repeated theme of Ravitch and Finn (and the vast majority of educators) is that by directing reading they are enabling children to distinguish what is valuable from what is not, what is "fine [from] what is dross."[39] But they have no more justification for their views than Mann had for his. Their assessments of value are no more insightful than their views about communication. While they claim to be providing children with the sensitivity to make fine-grained distinctions, they reveal themselves to be painting reality with a very broad brush.

[38]Jonathan Messerli, *Horace Mann: A Biography* (New York: Alfred A. Knopf, 1972), p. 346.

[39]Ravitch and Finn, p. 253.

Ravitch and Finn lament that young people know little about the important figures in history. The attention of students has been focused instead on "celebrities from *People* magazine and the electronic media" and "figures in sports and other realms of transitory achievement."[40]

Susan is a 15-year-old girl I have known since she was three. She is bright, vivacious, caring, interesting, fun to talk with. Reading books assigned by school has never been one of her favorite activities. A month ago I saw her glumly reading George Eliot's *The Mill on the Floss*. It took her two weeks of sullen effort. She was hardly able to get herself to sit down with it. Last Saturday we went to a library book sale and she bought fourteen books. By Sunday evening she had finished one of them, Gilda Radner's autobiography, *It's Always Something*. Perhaps Ravitch and Finn would say, "That is exactly why we have to monitor Susan and make sure that she reads what is worthwhile and beneficial. Left to herself, she read about an entertainer, someone from one of those realms of transitory achievement. What will that prepare her for—reading the *Enquirer*? It will certainly not prepare her to join in the debates others are having."

Susan spoke to me about the Gilda Radner book. She had been impressed, but not by something transitory and frivolous. What she was most affected by was a woman's courage in the face of death, an awesome struggle with a universal aspect of life. It was heroism of the highest sort that drew Susan's attention. Gilda Radner may not be enough of a heroine for Ravitch and Finn, but that is just one more reason for disregarding their prescriptions.

Many people could tell a similar story. One of mine involves Lou Gehrig. Growing up as a Yankee fan, I went to games, listened to them on the radio, read the sports page, and read about the history of the team. Of the players from the past, the one I admired the most and enjoyed reading about the most was Lou Gehrig. Like Susan with Gilda Radner, I was awed by his character, in particular the largeness of spirit displayed in the famous speech in which, knowing he was dying, he described himself as "the luckiest man on the face of the earth." I felt, and still do, that something transcendental was involved. Should one have regard for the educator who says that that is ephemeral and not worth attending to?

[40]Ibid., pp. 20, 216.

The situation with respect to reading in school is this: You must read something because some "experts" have said it will be meaningful to you. If you are getting nothing out of it, if it doesn't resonate in any way in your spirit, that makes no difference to them. You must go on with it and pay close attention. I think many people would prefer to read what they find interesting, even if they had to do it with a piece of paper in their mouths.

Reading is something that can and does enter many human lives in a lovely way, answering individual needs and questions, touching particular emotions. It is when the experts take over—and push and prod and direct and punish—that the dreadful atmosphere surrounding reading is created. H. L. Mencken sized up the situation this way:

> Is anything really valuable ever learned at school? I sometimes doubt it. Moreover, many wiser men doubt it, though they commonly make an exception of reading and writing. . . . I go further. I believe that even in the matter of reading and writing children commonly teach themselves, or one another. . . .
>
> There should be more sympathy for school-children. The idea that they are happy is of a piece with the idea that the lobster in the pot is happy. They are, in more ways than one, the worst and most pathetic victims of the complex of inanities and cruelties called civilization.[41]

What contributes to learning to read and to enjoyment in reading is an approach that is just the opposite of what one finds generally in the schools. The evidence shows, Raymond and Dorothy Moore write, that adults "who care, who respond warmly and consistently, who thus create an environment conducive to reading and support children's efforts, greatly facilitate children's learning to read. Motivation of this kind evidently does more for children's reading than exerting undue pressure to achieve or conducting special early school or other training programs. . . . With perceptual integration and maturation, most children have little difficulty with reading."[42]

[41]Mencken, p. 310.
[42]Moore and Moore, pp. 105–6.

Learning to Read

Many people learn to read on their own. That is an enjoyable, even a delightful experience, without book reports and identification quizzes. There are places of reading instruction for people who require more formal tutoring. But such places teach reading. They do not force people to read this or that on the alleged grounds that it will make them critical thinkers or that it will improve their ability to understand what others are debating. They are not trying to shape and direct mental or moral growth. They do not assume the authority to tell you what is worthwhile and what is not. People can learn to read, whether on their own or with instruction, without the comprehensive control of their lives that the reading curriculum represents.

In that regard educators could profit from the wisdom of one of their own favorites, Ralph Waldo Emerson.

> The secret of Education lies in respecting the pupil. It is not for you to choose what he shall know, what he shall do. . . . By your tampering and thwarting and too much governing he may be hindered from his end and kept out of his own. Respect the child. Wait and see the new product of Nature. Nature loves analogies, but not repetitions.
>
> Nature, when she sends a new mind into the world, fills it . . . with a desire for that which she wishes it to know and do. Let us wait and see what is this new creation, of what new organ the great Spirit had need when it incarnated this new Will. A new Adam in the garden, he is to name all the beasts in the field, all the gods in the sky. And jealous provision seems to have been made in his constitution that you shall not invade and contaminate him with the worn weeds of your language and opinions. The charm of life is this variety of genius, these contrasts and flavors by which Heaven has modulated the identity of truth, and there is a perpetual hankering to violate this individuality, to warp his ways of thinking and behavior to resemble or reflect your thinking and behavior. . . . I suffer whenever I see that common sight of a parent or senior imposing his opinion and way of thinking and being on a young soul to which they are totally unfit. Cannot we let people be themselves, and enjoy life in their own way? You are trying to make that man another you. One's enough.[43]

[43]Ralph Waldo Emerson, "Education," in *The Portable Emerson*, ed. Mark Van Doren (New York: Viking, 1946), pp. 256, 260.

Reading, like mathematics, is of great importance in human life. But, just as they do with mathematics, educators distort its role. They force children to master an arbitrary selection of mathematical techniques, claiming to be empowering the mind to think rationally. They force children to read an arbitrary selection of books, claiming to be empowering the mind to distinguish what is valuable from what is not. Those claims are both false. They issue from simplistic, limiting conceptions of rationality and value. They are, I believe, among the fundamental falsehoods responsible for the immense unhappiness of schooling.

5. Why Educational Reforms Have Failed

It has not gone unnoticed that much of schooling consists of requiring children to perform pointless tasks. But attempts to reform the system have failed. Though the details have been different, they have failed for the same underlying reason. Each has sought to replace what was seen as the false agenda of schooling with a true agenda of its own. The new curricula, however, turn out to be at least as misguided as the old. In this chapter I will try to illustrate that point by looking at two of the most influential attempts at reforming school programs, progressivism and structuralism. Those reforms not only failed; they ended as objects of ridicule. There is something to be learned from those failures about the careless reasoning that has so often characterized the thinking of educators. There is something to be learned also about the casual way that educators have imposed profitless labor on children in school.

By the early 1900s there was widespread criticism of what had developed in 60 years of compulsory schooling. Schooling was denounced by numerous writers for many of the same reasons it is being denounced today, that is, its authoritarianism, its mechanical form of teaching, the emphasis on rote memory, the passivity of the children. Even within the educational establishment, unhappiness with the character of schooling was being expressed. Professors of educational science were calling public school "the listening regime," a place dominated by "fears, restraints, and long weary hours of suppression."[1]

Progressivism

One of the major consequences of that criticism was the emergence of the progressive movement in education. Basing their views on a

[1]Diane Ravitch, *The Troubled Crusade: American Education, 1945–1980* (New York: Basic Books, 1983), p. 50.

combination of the social ideals of John Dewey and the techniques of behaviorist psychology, the progressives called for major changes in both the mission and the methods of schooling. They insisted that the schools take a more active role in bringing about positive social change and, to that end, in forming the kind of people who would contribute to such change. The process of schooling, Dewey said, should "saturate the child with the spirit of service."[2] The progressives rejected what they derisively called "subject matter fixed in advance." Children should not spend hour after hour passively taking instruction. William Heard Kilpatrick, professor of education at Teacher's College, Columbia, advanced what was called the Project Method. At the heart of all learning, said Kilpatrick, is "the purposeful act."[3] Instead of simply listening, children should be engaged in projects designed to simulate real-life situations.

By 1940 progressivism had become the dominant view in colleges and graduate schools of education. The validity of progressive theories and methods, it was widely believed, had been demonstrated by scientifically discovered laws of learning. The view had so permeated the thinking of professional educators that it was generally not even referred to as "progressive" education but simply as "modern education" or "good educational practice."[4] And yet within the next 15 years, under a mounting barrage of criticism, the movement collapsed. In 1955 the Progressive Education Association was dissolved, and "educators who once prided themselves on their identification with progressivism as a symbol of modern thought now shunned the label."[5] There were several reasons for that dramatic development.

In the first place, it became clear to neutral observers that the Project Method did not have the predicted vitalizing effect. The projects tended to become as rigid and formal as the lessons they replaced.[6] Instead of moving mechanically through "subject matter fixed in advance," children were moving mechanically through

---

[2]Quoted in Lawrence A. Cremin, *The Transformation of the School* (New York: Vintage Books, 1964), p. 118.

[3]Quoted in ibid., p. 216.

[4]Ravitch, p. 43.

[5]Ibid., p. 78.

[6]Cremin, p. 223.

"projects structured in advance." The "purposeful act" turned out to be a kind of pseudoactivity in which the steps the child was to take were already laid out.

Criticism intensified when it emerged that the supposed scientific validation for progressivism was nonexistent. Skewed sampling techniques had been used, and the most fragmentary results had been announced as constituting complete confirmation of the supposed laws of learning underlying progressive methods. Historian Richard Hofstadter says that the progressives' "misuse of experimental evidence constitutes a major scandal in the history of educational thought."[7]

The final collapse of progressivism was brought on when the Project Method evolved into what was called "life-adjustment education," a development that caused progressive theory to be seen by many as a farce. At a conference of educators in 1947, it was decided that too much of schooling was devoted to arcane and irrelevant matters. The curriculum had to be revised, it was declared, in order to give children "the life-adjustment training they need and to which they are entitled as American citizens."[8] Life adjustment quickly became the fashion among educators. Scores of publications appeared, advocating the new approach. *Developing a Curriculum for Modern Living,* published by Teacher's College, Columbia, stated, "Fundamentally this concept of curriculum development is one in which the basic problems and situations of everyday living in our democracy, which are central in life itself, also become central in the education of learners."[9] The experts turned their attention next to identifying life's problems. But instead of seeing the absurdity of trying to produce a definitive account of life's problems, valid for every individual, the educators began to produce lists. A typical effort, that of the Illinois Curriculum Program, offered a list of "real-life problems of youth." The committee identified 55 problems, among them, "the problem of selecting a 'family dentist' and acquiring the habit of visiting him systematically"; "the problem of

---

[7]Richard Hofstadter, *Anti-Intellectualism in American Life* (New York: Alfred A. Knopf, 1963), p. 349.

[8]Arthur Bestor, *Educational Wastelands* (Urbana and Chicago: University of Illinois Press, 1953), p. 82.

[9]Quoted in ibid., p. 83.

improving one's personal appearance"; "the problem of acquiring the ability to distinguish right from wrong and to guide one's actions accordingly"; "the problem of developing one or more 'making things,' 'making it go,' or 'tinkering' hobbies"; "the problem of acquiring the ability to study and help solve economic, social, and political problems"; and "the problem of developing and maintaining wholesome boy-girl relationships."[10] The bizarre character of that list was not lost on critics. As one writer put it, "The first thing that strikes one on reading the list is the grotesque disproportion between the different problems presented. Trivia are elaborated beyond all reason, and substantial matters are lumped together in a very small number of separate items, thus reducing them to relative insignificance in the whole."[11]

Nevertheless, the program moved forward. In one high school, for example, students took a course on what is expected of a boy on a date. They examined such issues as "Do girls want to 'pet'?" and "Should you go in with a girl after a date (to raid the ice box)?" Another school introduced a course on "Developing an Effective Personality," which dealt with such matters as "what kind of clothing [is] appropriate, what shade of nail polish to wear, and how to improve one's appearance."[12]

Those, and other, similar, offerings were not in place very long before they resulted in a flood of savage criticism. In books such as *Educational Wastelands* by Arthur Bestor and *Quackery in the Public Schools* by Albert Lynd, it was charged that the professional educators, left unchecked to spin out their "'scientific'" theories, had produced something preposterous. The lofty ideals of public education had been reduced to philistine triviality, with the schools offering "everything except a course in how to come in out of the rain."[13]

The initial response of the progressives was to discount those reactions as coming from "enemies of education." The critics, it was held, "represent the same sort of reactionary trend that always springs up when a doctrine is gaining headway in the country. The astonishing thing is not the fact of the reaction but that it is so small

[10]Quoted in ibid.
[11]Quoted in ibid.
[12]Ravitch, p. 68.
[13]Ibid., p. 72.

and on the whole comes from such inconspicuous people."[14] But the reaction was not small. On the contrary, the absurdity of what the "experts" had come up with was apparent to everyone but the most committed.

It should be pointed out, however, that one explanation sometimes given for the failure of progressivism—that it was too "permissive" or too "individualistic"—is not accurate. While they used phrases like "the child-centered school," the progressives, with science allegedly on their side, approached children in an even more authoritarian spirit than had their traditionalist opponents. As one leading progressive theorist bluntly put it, echoing John Watson, schooling exists "for the purpose of controlling human behavior."[15] Under progressive direction, a Committee on Economy of Time in Education was formed. Its task was to determine scientifically what children should study and how they should study it. The committee's recommendations sought to control children's behavior down to the smallest detail, going so far as to prescribe the position a child should be in when writing: "Both forearms should rest on the desk for approximately three quarters of their length."[16] Scientific evidence had shown, the committee said, that "when one elbow [is] unsupported, spinal curvature [is] often the result."[17] In one school district run by progressives, it was decided that the schools should know "what every single child in the community between 6 and 18 is doing with his life in school, before school, and after school, and even during summer vacation."[18] A school nurse was sent to grade every home on "thrift, neatness, cleanliness, income, health, harmony or discord, presence of reading matter, and make, type, and year of automobile."[19]

By the mid-1950s it had become clear to virtually everyone that the progressive movement represented, not a scientific understanding of how to help children, but rather a "pretentious scientism."[20] The

[14]Ibid., p. 59.
[15]Quoted in ibid., p. 60.
[16]Cremin, p. 196.
[17]Ibid.
[18]Ravitch, p. 57.
[19]Ibid.
[20]Ibid., p. 46.

journal of the movement, *Progressive Education*, folded in 1957, by which time the very expression "progressive education" had changed from a term of praise to one of ridicule.

Structuralism

The collapse of progressivism was closely followed by a new call for reform, also representing itself as scientific, but with quite different recommendations. In May 1959 a group of educators convened in Woods Hole, Massachusetts, under the chairmanship of Professor Jerome Bruner, director of the Center for Cognitive Studies at Harvard University. The group consisted of specialists in various academic disciplines, along with educational psychologists. The aim was to produce a plan for replacing the lifeless school curriculum with one possessing vitality and meaning.

The conclusions of the Woods Hole conference were presented in Bruner's *The Process of Education* and *Toward a Theory of Instruction*. When they appeared, those books were widely praised as marking a turning point in the scientific understanding of how children should be taught. Bruner, it was said, had stirred up more excitement than any educator since John Dewey. Many of the recommended programs were implemented in schools across the country. But the new reform had an even shorter life than its progressive predecessor. Within a decade, enthusiasm had faded on the part of everyone but the original core group, and the reform was seen as a misguided failure. All of the programs were cancelled, having been declared not only useless but even psychologically harmful. Once again "educational science" had led to the imposition of profitless activities on children.

The members of the Woods Hole conference, like the progressives, were severe in their condemnation of traditional schooling. They saw it as largely wasted labor. School mathematics, Bruner said, was "little but memory and computation." Social studies was nothing but a "congeries of facts." As for grammar, it was simply "deadening."[21] The reason those studies have no value, Bruner said, is that they don't give children any genuine understanding. The child is not provided with a framework, a structure to hold things together.

---

[21]Jerome Bruner, *Toward a Theory of Instruction* (New York: W. W. Norton, 1966), p. 76.

Disconnected facts are meaningless. They will inevitably, Bruner said, have a "pitiably short half-life in memory."[22] If children are to acquire understanding, they must be introduced, as early as possible, to the "fundamental structure" of the various disciplines they study. Armed with the fundamental structure—of mathematics, social studies, biology, history, and so forth—the child supposedly will have a conceptual framework within which the individual facts can take on meaning.

From the outset there was considerable skepticism about the structuralist reform. Critics said that the program would not help children; it would only confuse them with ideas they would be in no position to understand. Bruner and his colleagues, buttressed by their "scientific" knowledge, were undeterred. In what became the slogan of the structuralist reform, Bruner declared, "Any subject can be taught to any child at any age in some form that is honest."[23] But that was a complete misperception, as the brief history of structuralism shows.

The most widely implemented part of the program, and its most conspicuous failure, was the so-called new math. Underlying that reform was the conviction, shared by Bruner's group and several other educational committees, that traditional school mathematics fails to give children a mathematical education. It merely trains them to carry out mechanical computational procedures. If children are to understand mathematics, they have to understand its fundamental concepts, in particular, the concept of number. Mathematics, as it has been taught, makes it impossible to understand the concept of number. In fact, it makes the concept of number unintelligible by confusing numbers with numerals. As one leading proponent of the new math put it, "It is our contention that in the exposition of elementary and secondary mathematics there is so much confusion of names with their referents that in many cases the student has never discovered that there is a distinction between symbols and their referents. . . . An exposition which is guilty of this confusion is just about useless."[24]

[22]Jerome Bruner, *The Process of Education* (Cambridge, Mass.: Harvard University Press, 1960), p. 31.

[23]Ibid., p. ix.

[24]Max Beberman, "An Emerging Program of Secondary School Mathematics," in *Education in the United States: A Documentary History*, ed. Sol Cohen (New York: Random House, 1974), p. 3237.

In teaching the new math, central importance was given to making clear to children that, strictly speaking, "3" is not a number. It is a numeral, a symbol that refers to a number. The same number can also be referred to in different ways, for example, III, iii, 8 − 5. Numbers, it was explained, are entities of a more abstract sort than numerals; they are sets. "Consider the . . . child who notices that to dress her three dolls she must have three dresses, three hats, three parasols, and three pairs of shoes. Her awareness of the class of sets of three things is an awareness of an entity. The entity is the number three and a name of the entity is the word three. . . . To say that a child understands the number three is to say that the child is aware of this class of matching sets."[25]

To enable children to understand that mathematics deals with classes of matching sets, the terminology of set theory was introduced. Instead of speaking of "the values of x that satisfy x + 3 = 5," children were taught to call such an expression an "open sentence" and to ask for the "truth set" of that open sentence. Mathematical operations such as addition, subtraction, and multiplication were reformulated in terms of set unions, set intersections, and so on. That recasting of mathematics required introducing a new notation for writing mathematical formulas and a large array of abstract concepts: null set, set union, set intersection, open phrase, open sentence, solution set.

Those changes did not have the intended effect. The distinction between numbers and numerals, and the importance of strictly observing the distinction, was lost on children. Instead of advancing their understanding of mathematics, the profusion of technical jargon left them more confused by mathematics than ever. And, critics charged, there was no good reason for it in the first place. The Nobel laureate physicist Richard Feynman, in a survey of new math textbooks, wrote,

> A zookeeper, instructing his assistant to take the sick lizards out of the cage, could say, "Take that set of animals which is the intersection of the set of lizards with the set of sick animals out of the cage." This language is correct, precise, set theoretical language, but it says no more than "Take the sick lizards out of the cage." . . . It will perhaps surprise

[25]Ibid.

most people who have studied these textbooks to discover
that the symbol "∪" or "∩" representing union and intersection of sets and the special use of brackets and so forth, all
the elaborate notation for sets that is given in these books,
almost never appear in any writing in theoretical physics, in
engineering, in business arithmetic, computer design, or
other places where mathematics is being used. I see no need
or reason for all this to be explained or to be taught in school.
It is not a useful way to express one's self. It is not a cogent
and simple way. It is claimed to be precise, but precise for
what purpose? . . . Many of the math books that are suggested
now are full of such nonsense—of carefully and precisely
defined special words that are used by pure mathematicians
in their most subtle and difficult analyses, and are used by
nobody else. . . . The real problem in speech is not precise
language. The problem is clear language.[26]

Not only did the new terminology fail to clarify the concept of
number, but the children did not, in any meaningful sense, learn it.
They memorized the definitions for the exams, but it was apparent,
to everyone but the reformers, that the children were not able to
use the concepts they had been trained to produce. The rote memorizing of traditional mathematics had been replaced by the rote
memorizing of set theory. Within 10 years of its introduction, the
new math had landed on the pile of educational discards.

Structuralism in social studies produced a similar result. The social
studies course, intended for children in the fifth grade, was developed by Bruner, along with several of his colleagues. Its title was
"Man: A Course of Study," and, in its pilot phase, it was taught by
Bruner himself. It was supposed to be different from traditional
social studies courses. Above all, it was not to be a "congeries of
facts." "We should like," Bruner wrote, "to make the study more
rational, more amenable to the use of mind in the large rather than
mere memorizing."[27] The purpose of the course was not to foist
information on children but to be an investigation in which the
child "masters himself, disciplines his taste, deepens his view of the

[26]Quoted in Morris Kline, *Why Johnny Can't Add: The Failure of the New Math* (New York: Vintage Books, 1974), pp. 87–88.
[27]Bruner, *Toward a Theory of Instruction*, p. 96.

world."[28] In practice, however, MACOS (as it was known under the government grant funding it) descended rapidly from those lofty goals into technical jargon and unintelligibility.

The course set out to investigate various factors that have contributed to human development, such as toolmaking, social organization, and language. In order for children to understand the role of language in human development, Bruner said, they must first be taught what a language is. And so, as a necessary preliminary to further investigation, he began by attempting to teach the fundamentals of linguistics.

The opening session on linguistics was devoted to explaining the properties of communication systems in general. Among the matters considered were "how one refers by signs and symbols to 'things,' the difficulties of reference when what is referred to is not present to point to, the relative advantages of a voice-ear system, the difference between an inherited and a culturally transmitted language."[29]

It is difficult to credit the claim that so much was discussed in that first session. Like Dr. Boyer, president of the Carnegie Foundation for the Advancement of Teaching, Professor Bruner seemed to be overstating what his course accomplished. How could so many complicated issues have been discussed, in an hour, with 10-year-old children who were, moreover, hearing about those matters for the first time in their lives? One can see here already why the fate of the new math was repeated, why the children were unable to use those concepts in any meaningful way.

That becomes more apparent when one looks at how the course proceeded and the concepts piled up. Having supposedly explained the notions of signs, symbols, and linguistic reference, Bruner next presented "the powerful idea of productivity." That was done by using

> a lexicon containing four word classes (how, what, when, and where words), with a limited number of tokens of each type (by hand, by weapon, by trap, are tokens of the "how" type), and we use word-class order to refer to different food-related activities. By this means we readily establish the notion of word type and order as two basic ideas. . . . We

[28]Ibid., p. 71.
[29]Ibid., p. 77.

hope to . . . help the children discover . . . that one can start
with relatively simple sentence frames, "kernel sentences,"
and transform them successively into negatives, queries, and
passives, or any two or even three of these, and that more
complex forms can be returned to simpler forms by applying
the transformations in reverse.[30]

That was followed by a session on morphemics in which Bruner
explained that "each human language combines intrinsically meaningless sounds into a unique system of phonemes that make up
words or morphemes."[31] He "clarified" those ideas by having the
children engage in an exercise in which

> we construct a language initially with a very limited set of
> phonemes as our building blocks. Three kinds of blocks can
> be arranged in various ways in a three-block frame, making
> twenty-seven possible "words" or morphemes. It is very
> quickly apparent to the children that the blocks as such
> "mean" nothing, but the frames do—or some do and some
> do not. We go from here to more complex notions of morpho-
> phonemics if the children are interested.[32]

In the next session Bruner made use of "the considerable resources
provided by recent studies of language acquisition to show the
manner in which syntax emerges from certain very elementary
forms."[33] Finally,

> with the benefit of the children's increased insight into the
> nature of language, we return to the question of the origins
> and functions of human language and the role of language
> in shaping human characteristics and thought. We . . . cover
> the newly available materials on the universal characteristics
> of all human languages—encouraging the children to make
> informed guesses on the subject.[34]

What is most striking about that account is the degree of self-
deception it reveals. Bruner was mistaken in thinking that he provided the children with increased insight into the nature of language.

[30]Ibid., p. 78.
[31]Ibid., p. 79.
[32]Ibid.
[33]Ibid., p. 80.
[34]Ibid.

What he did was take them on a confusing whirlwind tour through a labyrinth of abstract concepts: sign, symbol, type, token, kernel sentence, elementary syntactic form, sentence frame, linguistic transformation. Having done that, he deluded himself into thinking that the children were in a position to make informed guesses on the universal characteristics of all human languages.

The children did not begin to understand what he was talking about. And how could they? The ideas he brought up are among the most difficult and perplexing in the history of human thought. The concept of linguistic reference, for example, has been addressed by every great philosopher from Plato to Wittgenstein, and there is still no generally accepted analysis. One cannot simply dish out abstract ideas like spaghetti and expect the recipient to be nourished. "Premature abstractions fall on deaf ears," Morris Kline rightly observed.[35] And that is exactly what happened in Bruner's class. The children were turned off and they resisted his lessons. "Getting children to look at and ponder the things they can notice in their language," Bruner said ruefully, "is most difficult."[36]

Like many educators, Bruner thought the difficulty was the fault of the children. He found them "lazy in using information, not exploiting its inferential power to nearly the degree warranted."[37] That is a radical misperception of the situation. Those children were not lazy. In fact, the children selected to participate in his pilot class, Bruner said, had come from especially stimulating home backgrounds where particular emphasis had been placed on intellectual achievement.[38] Nevertheless, they were repelled by all his unintelligible verbiage.

Surprisingly, and despite his experience, Bruner pronounced MACOS a success. He had demonstrated, he said, that "these matters can be presented to children in a fashion that is gripping, close to life, and intellectually honest."[39] One is hard-pressed to think of anything to which that description would be less appropriate. And Bruner knew that that was so. He knew that the children didn't

[35]Kline, p. 119.
[36]Bruner, *Toward a Theory of Instruction*, p. 77.
[37]Ibid., p. 99.
[38]Ibid., p. 58.
[39]Ibid., p. 84.

find it gripping. Holding their interest in the relationship between phonemes and morphemes or in the emergence of syntax from elementary forms turned out to be impossible. A crucial task for educational experts, Bruner said, is to find out how to "inure the child to longer and longer episodes of learning."[40] Perhaps only in the somewhat dizzying world of educational theorizing could one come across the claim that human beings have to become inured to what they find gripping.

But, gripping or not, why should the teaching of linguistics have been undertaken in the first place? Why did Bruner think it necessary to provide 10-year-old children with what he calls "the self-conscious understanding of the linguist"? It must be done, he said, because

> if there is not a developed awareness of the different func-
> tions that language serves, the resulting affliction will be not
> only lopsided speaking and writing, but a lopsided mind. . . .
> The afflicted person will be restricted in coping to events for
> which his stunted language provides suitable equipment.
> And one day he may be forced to fight a forest fire with a
> water pistol.[41]

Here once again is the characteristic claim of the educator, that disaster will befall those who don't have what he has discovered to be indispensable. They will be reduced to coping with life in a primitive, barbaric way. But Bruner's claim of indispensability has a hollow ring. The facts certainly don't support it. There are many people whose minds are not lopsided but who also have nothing of "the self-conscious understanding of the linguist." There are people whose language is not at all stunted, people who speak well and even beautifully, who are completely innocent of the relationship between phonemes and morphemes, and who, if they had to explain under pressure how syntax emerged from elementary forms, could only cough and stammer.

Bruner and his team of educational experts reversed the truth. Something altogether unnecessary was imposed on children on the grounds that it is indispensable. What was offered as a path to an understanding of the nature of language, and via that to an

[40]Bruner, *The Process of Education*, p. 50.
[41]Bruner, *Toward a Theory of Instruction*, pp. 109–10.

understanding of human nature, was nothing but a mass of indigestible technical jargon. There were definitions to be memorized and exercises to be carried out—an enormous amount of mental movement going nowhere. Not surprisingly, what the children learned was found by independent observers to be "limited in scope, to lack permanence, and to be of little benefit to the child."[42] To call it a substantial contribution to forming the intellectual powers, as Bruner did, is far from the truth.

Also untrue is the claim that the structuralist reform was based on scientific knowledge about human mental development. As the progressives did with their programs, Bruner spoke of "psychological experts" and "scientific theories of learning" supporting the structuralist curriculum. But when it came to determining what children should be required to study, his criterion was not scientific at all. Ask of any subject, he said, if it is "when fully developed . . . worth an adult's knowing."[43] One sees here that the basis of the program had nothing to do with any scientific theory of learning or any theory about the causes of mental "lopsidedness." The structuralist curriculum was based on nothing more than the opinion of Bruner and his colleagues that what it contained was worth knowing. It may be that a majority of the members of the Woods Hole conference agreed that morphemics is gripping. But, like educators in general, they made the mistake of forcing their taste onto unwilling others—and calling it science.

Both progressivism and structuralism began with insight. In many respects their analyses of schooling could not have been more accurate. The progressives claimed that passively receiving information all day long about innumerable "subject matters fixed in advance" is mind numbing. And that is true. The structuralists said that disconnected facts are empty. And that is true. But in each case the reformers were unable to look at their own programs in the same critical spirit. As a consequence, they deceived themselves into believing that they had discovered a general method of developing the mind, a method that should be imposed on every child. The results did

[42]Raymond S. Moore and Dorothy N. Moore, *School Can Wait* (Provo, Utah: Brigham Young University Press, 1979), p. 134.

[43]Bruner, *The Process of Education*, p. 52.

not, as was intended, replace the lifelessness of schooling with vitality and meaning and benefit. Instead, one form of misdirection was replaced by another.

The failure of those reforms has led, in recent years, to a resurgence of "traditionalism" in educational theorizing. The next chapter will examine that reaction.

6. On Memorizing

If any aspect of schooling has been singled out for special condemnation, it is the enormous amount of time and energy devoted to the memorizing of information: dates of battles, provisions of treaties, mathematical formulas, chemical valences, names of bones, stages of cell division, principal crops, and so on. Such information, for all the effort required to absorb it, has, as Professor Bruner says, "a pitiably short half-life in memory."[1]

Recently, however, numerous educators have claimed that forcing children to memorize large amounts of information is a good thing. The most influential of those educators, E. D. Hirsch Jr., professor of English at the University of Virginia, in his book *Cultural Literacy*, contends that the schools are not requiring children to memorize enough. Children should be "piling up information," Hirsch says. The opposition to rote memorizing, he insists, is "more pious than realistic."[2]

Is that true? Does a "realistic" approach to children support rote memorizing? When looked at in detail, Hirsch's claims turn out to be filled with the same kind of exaggeration and distortion that is characteristic of so much of educational thinking.

Hirsch's defense of rote memorizing rests on the surprising claim that to become a competent reader and speaker of one's native language one must be, in his phrase, "culturally literate." To be culturally literate, Hirsch says, is to be in possession of a certain body of "specific information."[3] That claim is surprising in that it conflicts with what is perhaps the most firmly established fact concerning the acquisition of linguistic ability, namely, that people

[1]Jerome Bruner, *The Process of Education* (Cambridge, Mass.: Harvard University Press, 1960), p. 31.

[2]E. D. Hirsch Jr., *Cultural Literacy: What Every American Needs to Know* (Boston: Houghton Mifflin, 1987), p. 30.

[3]Ibid., p. 19.

with widely different experiences, attitudes, and information become competent readers and speakers of their native language. As Noam Chomsky puts it, "Great diversity of input conditions does not lead to a wide diversity in resulting competence."[4] Indeed, a major task of the science of linguistics, according to Chomsky, is to account for that fact about language acquisition.

Hirsch denies that. He insists that "one literate person knows approximately the same things as another."[5] But surely that claim is false. Literate people, it seems obvious, know vastly different things: Jones has a special interest in Renaissance art, Smith in baseball, Brown in horticulture, Kaplan in politics, and so on. That there is a determinate body of information possessed by all literate people is not a realistic assumption on which to base a theory of education.

Fortunately, it is possible to examine Hirsch's claim more directly, for he contends not only that there is such a definite body of information that all competent readers possess, but that its contents "can be identified explicitly."[6] As a result of "research in the field," he says, he has actually been able to come up with a list, which he provides. The list contains a varied assortment of items. There are presidents, generals, baseball players, cities, movie stars, song titles, proverbs, dates, explorers, and philosophical theories. His list, he says, is "a fairly reliable index to the . . . information that is shared by most literate people but remains largely unfamiliar to most illiterate people."[7]

If one looks at Hirsch's fact list, it is immediately apparent that what he says is not true. There are many widely familiar items on the list: Abraham Lincoln, Shakespeare, and South Dakota. But the list also includes Marianas Trench, sinking fund, Christopher Wren, and the principle of mathematical induction. It is a considerable distortion of the truth to say that all competent readers are familiar with those items.

Hirsch has not provided a list of what literate people know. His is a list of what he thinks they ought to know. Hirsch denies that also.

---

[4]Noam Chomsky, "Recent Contributions to the Theory of Innate Ideas," in *The Philosophy of Language*, ed. J. R. Searle (London: Oxford University Press, 1971), p. 122.

[5]Hirsch, p. 16.

[6]Ibid., p. 134.

[7]Ibid.

His list, he claims, is descriptive, not prescriptive. It does nothing but describe "common knowledge."[8] One wonders how that can be said of a list containing Artemis, Ceres, titration, and noble gas.

Hirsch misrepresents the character of his fact list in other ways as well. The reason children should be required to know what is on it, he says, is that the list represents "the national vocabulary." It contains "the instruments through which we communicate our views."[9] But again, that is a claim that has very little to do with reality. Some views, of course, are communicated using items on the list. But many views are communicated using information that has nothing to do with that list. Hirsch's list is no more than a tiny slice of the national vocabulary. Were the instruments of communication restricted to what Hirsch offers, people could say very little of what they want to say. They couldn't talk about Afghanistan or Monaco or moonshine or mononucleosis or hypocrisy or depression or Dorothea Dix or Simón Bolívar or Friedrich Schiller or Goliath or the Caspian Sea or Héloïse and Abelard or vampires or orangutans or May Day or POWs or the Last Judgment. Calling what he offers "the national vocabulary" would seem to be nothing but presumption on Hirsch's part.

Hirsch goes on to make even grander claims about his list. He calls it an ordered "network of associations," acquaintance with which provides "a profound conception of the whole civilization."[10] But order is precisely what his list lacks. On the contrary, it appears to be a structureless collection of names.

In every area the list touches, the selections made are arbitrary. For example, the names of various cities are on the list. But it is entirely a mystery why some names are included and others left out. Thus, Naples is on the list but Bologna is not. Calcutta is on the list but Calais is not. Birmingham, Alabama, is on the list, as is Manchester, England, though Birmingham, England, is not. Buffalo, New York, makes the list. Failing to make it, however, are Wilmington and Tallahassee and Odessa and Milan. And so on.

Baptist is on the list but Methodist isn't. Neither is Amish, though Mennonite is.

[8]Ibid., p. 107.
[9]Ibid., pp. 139, 107.
[10]Ibid., p. 10.

Plato, Aristotle, Hobbes, Hegel, and Wittgenstein are all on the list. But Kierkegaard and Schopenhauer are not.

Ginger Rogers is on the list.

Mozambique is on the list, but Tanzania isn't, though Tasmania is, followed by Tchaikovsky and Teenybopper.

Hirsch addressed some of the failings in the subsequently published *Dictionary of Cultural Literacy*. The new list, however, is no less arbitrary than the original one. It is just another random collection of names and facts, expressing no discernible vision, profound or otherwise.

That the list is arbitrary is concealed by, and perhaps from, Hirsch by his use of "scientific" language. He claims to have discovered the "critical mass of information" required for literacy.[11] Such a discovery would be of monumental importance, with far-reaching implications. But Hirsch is merely playing at science. He has not made any discovery at all. There is no scientific law relating the possession of his information to the ability to read, despite his claim that his proposal is supported by "empirical psychology."[12] And there could be no such law, since there is no such relation. To describe one's subjective, limited outlook using scientific language does not make what one says scientific. Hirsch has presented something that is purely subjective and arbitrary as though it were objective and ordered. The only order possessed by Professor Hirsch's fact list is alphabetical.

With the lack of restraint characteristic of educators praising their own programs, Hirsch goes so far as to say that knowing what is on his list is necessary if a child is going to become an autonomous human being. We should be encouraged by that discovery of his, he maintains, since it means that "only a few hundred pages of information stand between . . . dependence and autonomy."[13]

Were that true, were there so much power in his list, perhaps there would be a justification for forcing children to memorize what is on it. Hirsch's claim, however, is not only untrue; it is absurd. It is not an insightful conception that finds the essence of human autonomy in an arbitrarily constructed fact list.

[11]Ibid., p. 144.
[12]Ibid., p. 62.
[13]Ibid., p. 143.

One sees here again the characteristic pattern of educational theorizing, groundless claims that some activity or other is indispensable for children's mental development. A fact list is declared by an educator to be the essence of autonomy, and so something children "need to know." That is a prelude to meaningless activity. Its end result is not autonomy but classes like the world history class described by Dr. Boyer. Or an educator says that children need to become acquainted with "the problem-solving process"—and then years of math puzzles ensue. Or the tedium of memorizing French verb endings is imposed on children because "they need to understand other nations in our increasingly interdependent world."

When the path to individual autonomy is represented as being paved with the memorizing of items on a fact list, reality is being distorted. Human life is too rich and subtle to be dealt with in such a crude way. At least this much is true: whenever such rhetorical nonsense is endorsed, and then imposed on every child, one can be sure that the individual development and growth of children are not being encouraged.

7. Shaping Human Beings and Pseudoscience

Educators have had widely divergent ideas about what should be taught in school and how it should be taught. What they have not disagreed about is that their task is to shape children, to shape their cognitive faculties, their curiosity, their moral character. Horace Mann wrote, "No idea can be more erroneous than that children go to school to learn the rudiments of knowledge only, and not to form character."[1] John Dewey said that education is the science of the formation of character.[2] Professor Jerome Bruner says that his aim is to shape the curiosity of the child, to manage the child's mental development.[3] Unless they are shaped, according to that view, children—and the adults they are going to become—will suffer from a variety of afflictions; they will be illogical or uncurious or lopsided or barbaric.

That idea reflects a way of thinking about children that long antedates formal schooling. The history of adult interaction with children has been one of molding and shaping, of both the body and the mind. One had to impose a proper shape on the child, it was long believed, in order to counteract the child's own inherently evil nature. In a 17th-century book of advice to parents, *A Godly Form of Household Government*, the authors wrote, "The young child which lieth in the cradle is both wayward and full of affections; and though his body be but small, yet he hath a reat [wrong-doing] heart, and is altogether inclined to evil. . . . If this sparkle be suffered to increase, it will rage over and burn down the whole house."[4]

[1] Horace Mann, *Lectures and Annual Reports on Education*, ed. Mary Mann (Cambridge, Mass.: Published for the editor, 1867), p. 119.

[2] John Dewey, "What Psychology Can Do for the Teacher," in *John Dewey on Education*, ed. Reginald Archambault (Chicago: University of Chicago Press, 1964), p. 197.

[3] Jerome Bruner, *Toward a Theory of Instruction* (New York: W. W. Norton, 1966), p. 73.

[4] Robert Cleaver and John Dod, *A Godly Form of Household Government*, quoted in Joseph E. Illick, "Child-Rearing in Seventeenth-Century England and America," in *The History of Childhood*, ed. Lloyd deMause (New York: Psychohistory Press, 1974), p. 316.

The child's evil nature manifested itself in a variety of ways, among them, a tendency of the body toward lopsided growth. The countermeasure was swaddling. Children were wrapped tightly to ensure that their bodily development would be "straight." A 17th-century child expert advised parents that the child's arms and legs should be "stretched strait" and wrapped tightly to the body. The child's head was to be immobilized with a stay fastened on each side of the blanket. It was necessary for the child to be swaddled in that way "to give his little body a strait Figure, which is most decent and convenient for a Man and to accustom him to keep upon the Feet, for else he would go upon all fours as most other Animals do."[5]

The shaping of the child's moral nature was carried out by instilling fear. The ancient Greeks used monsters such as Gorgon and Sybaris to frighten children into proper behavior. It was thought to be good for children to have the images of monsters constantly before them, to be terrorized by the thought of those creatures kidnapping them and tearing them to pieces or sucking out their blood. In the medieval period, writes historian Lloyd deMause, "witches and devils took front stage, with an occasional Jew thrown in as a cutter of babies' throats."[6]

That way of thinking about how to shape a child's moral nature was reflected in the way children were treated in school. As late as the mid-19th century, classes were taken to see hangings, after which they were given moral instruction. Parents, too, brought their children to hangings and would then whip them so that the event would remain fixed in their minds.

Swaddling children and terrorizing them, as methods of shaping, began to come under attack during the Enlightenment. John Locke called swaddling a misguided assault on children. And he pointed out that in Sparta, where swaddling was not practiced, children not only developed normally but walked earlier than children in

[5]François Mauriceau, *Diseases of Women with Child and in Child-Bed* (Paris: 1668; London: 1727), quoted in G. F. Still, *The History of Pediatrics* (London: Oxford University Press, 1931), p. 390.

[6]Lloyd deMause, "The Evolution of Childhood," in *The History of Childhood*, p. 11.

swaddling societies.[7] Locke also condemned the practice of terrorizing children into moral behavior.

The change that followed, however, was not a fundamental change in attitude toward children but rather one of method of control. According to the new, "enlightened," approach, children were not to be frightened, but rather shamed, into acceptable behavior. Locke says that "if you can once get into children a love of credit and an apprehension of shame and disgrace, you have put into them the true principle, which will constantly work, and incline them to the right."[8] That attitude was reflected in the schools. One should not terrify children, teachers were advised, but rather train them by "punishing misdeeds in such a way as to give them a little honest shame to have committed them rather than too much fear of punishment. . . . We are impelled only by . . . the desire to render them such as God wishes them."[9]

The practices that emerged from that new conception were hardly an improvement over the images of monsters. Teachers in one school, for example, were told to make placards for the children on which their faults were described in large letters: "lazy," "negligent," "liar."

Whether the means involved terror or shame, the goal in dealing with children remained the same. It was to exercise total control over the child's mental and spiritual development. What was demanded of the child was a "hearty submission," a "perfect subordination."[10] The training of children, Locke said, must be "begun early, and inflexibly kept to, till . . . there appears not the least reluctancy in the submission and ready obedience of their minds."[11] Adults "should carefully subdue the wills of their children," wrote one child expert, "and accustom them to obedience and submission."[12] No one put the point more vividly than the German

[7]John Locke, *Some Thoughts Concerning Education,* in *On Politics and Education,* ed. Howard R. Penniman (New York: D. Van Nostrand, 1947), § 12, p. 216.

[8]Ibid., § 56, p. 241.

[9]deMause, pp. 277, 279.

[10]Ibid., p. 361.

[11]Locke, § 44, p. 237.

[12]John Bernard, *A Call to Parents and Children* (Boston: 1773), quoted in John F. Walzer, "A Period of Ambivalence: Eighteenth-Century American Childhood," in *The History of Childhood,* p. 365.

philosopher Johann Gottlieb Fichte, whose ideas formed the philosophical foundation of Germany's educational system.

> Education must consist essentially in this, that it completely destroys freedom of will in the soil which it undertakes to cultivate, and produces on the contrary strict necessity in the decisions of the will, the opposite decision being impossible. Such a will can henceforth be relied on with confidence and certainty.... [Schooling] must fashion the person, and fashion him in such a way that he simply cannot will otherwise than what you wish him to will.... The education proposed by me, therefore, is to be a reliable and deliberate art for fashioning in man a stable and infallible good will.[13]

Historians of education have often claimed that the system of public schooling that Mann launched in Massachusetts represented a reaction against that kind of authoritarianism. It has been held to express a more insightful way of dealing with children, one that encourages independence of mind and not mere submission.

That view of the ideas underlying public schooling is erroneous. It is true that by the standards of his time Mann was forward looking. He campaigned against corporal punishment and he insisted that children be provided with more comfortable surroundings in school. But his conception of schooling and his view of children were essentially identical with those of earlier times. "From our very constitution," he said, "there is a downward gravitation to overcome.... Our propensities have no affinity with reason or conscience.... Hence these propensities require some mighty counterpoise to balance their proclivity to wrong."[14]

Schooling, Mann thought, is that counterpoise. Its mission is that of "ransoming the human race from its brutish instincts and demoniac indulgences."[15] To carry out that mission, the school must shape the child's character, a process that requires total control over the child. The teacher, Mann said, is "the will of the school." The students are "the body which that will moves."[16]

---

[13]Johann Gottlieb Fichte, *Addresses to the German Nation* (New York: Harper and Row, 1968), pp. 17–18.

[14]Mann, pp. 165, 195.

[15]Ibid., p. 199.

[16]Ibid., p. 137.

If there is anything "modern" about Mann's approach to children, it is his idea that in school children could be shaped scientifically, a claim since echoed by Dewey, Watson, Piaget, Bruner, and innumerable others. It is absolutely necessary, Mann said, for educators to have knowledge of the scientific laws governing children's mental development so that they will be able to direct that development properly. But, as noted earlier, Mann's claim that schooling is based on science was groundless. It was supported by nothing but the pseudoscience of phrenology.

The idea that schooling is a process of scientifically shaping the mind and character of children was not original with Mann. He gave political expression to a doctrine that was widely held in the 18th and 19th centuries, the doctrine that human beings in general, and children in particular, require "scientific shaping." In the wake of the revolution in the physical sciences—epitomized by Newton's discovery of the laws of motion—numerous philosophers began to claim that there were general laws of mental development, analogous to the laws of physics.

The French Enlightenment philosopher Condorcet, in his *Sketch of a Historical Picture of the Progress of the Human Mind*, said that just as there are general physical laws governing the operations of the material universe, so there must be general psychological laws governing the operations of the mind. What Condorcet, along with many others, derived from that idea was the notion of a comprehensive science of society, a science that could be used to direct and accelerate the progress of the human race. One could remake society, they believed, by remaking human beings, that is to say, by scientifically forming an individual's character on the basis of a knowledge of the general laws governing mental development.

That idea came to dominate social philosophy. Count Henri Saint-Simon, the first in a long line of French socialist thinkers, who had immersed himself in the thought of Condorcet, called for a complete reorganization of society so that everyone's behavior could be scientifically directed. There was to be no place for individuality in the new order. In Saint-Simon's vision, society would be run by scientific experts, governing through "Councils of Newton." The education of children would be part of the scientific plan.

But when one looks for the scientific truths on the basis of which all that was to be accomplished, they cannot be found. Instead one

finds merely Saint-Simon's views about what constitutes a worthy
and useful life, views that he declared to be both infallible and
obligatory.

> All men will work. They will regard themselves as laborers
> attached to one workshop whose efforts will be directed to
> guide human intelligence according to my divine foresight.
> The supreme Council of Newton will direct their works. . . .
> Anybody who does not obey the orders will be treated by
> the others as a quadruped.[17]

One sees here a vivid example of how pseudoscience leads to
authoritarianism.

Saint-Simon's disciple, Auguste Comte, the "father of sociology,"
developed the idea further. Comte claimed to have discovered a
"social physics" containing the laws of the development of the mind
and of society, laws that he said, in an obvious reference to Newton
and Galileo, were "as definite as those determining the fall of a
stone."[18] On the basis of a knowledge of those laws, one could assign
"to every individual . . . that precise kind of activity for which [he
or she is] fitted."[19] In Comte's view, a "Government of Opinion,"
consisting of "competent scientists," would determine "the entire
system of ideas and habits necessary for initiating individuals into
the social order under which they must live."[20] But Comte had no
scientific truths to offer. The "science" on the basis of which he
proposed to direct all human activity was the same science Mann
intended to use to direct the mental development of children,
phrenology.

There were scores of social theorists, from Saint-Simon to Marx
and beyond, each one proposing to shape people on the basis of his
alleged scientific insight into human nature and the path that must
be followed if a human being is to develop properly. But every one of
those schemes turned out to be based on nothing but pseudoscience.
When attempts were made to implement them, the result was
always failure.

[17]Quoted in F. A. Hayek, *The Counter-Revolution of Science* (Glencoe, Ill.: Free Press,
1952), p. 121.

[18]Quoted in ibid., p. 178.

[19]Quoted in ibid., p. 140.

[20]Quoted in ibid.

Perhaps the most well known 19th-century attempt was that of the English industrialist Robert Owen, founder of the "scientific" community at New Harmony, Indiana, in 1825. Owen's "new view of society" had its source in the same idea we have been describing, that by scientifically controlling the causes affecting people one could produce exactly the kind of individual one wanted. That could be done, Owen said, "with the certainty of a law of nature" and "with mathematical precision."[21]

Owen's belief that he possessed a scientific technique for shaping people was pure illusion. His "scientific method" consisted of nothing more than lecturing people about how he thought life ought to be lived. Every Wednesday evening the inhabitants of New Harmony were required to gather in the meeting hall to hear Owen speak. He believed that, since human beings are rational creatures, anyone exposed to the obvious rationality of his view of the good life would be converted. Children would not have to be converted. The new society would scientifically educate them in such a way that they would not even be able to imagine any other way of life.

For those who resisted scientific character formation, provision would be made. In a somewhat chilling anticipation of the future, Owen wrote,

> All individuals, trained, educated, and placed, in conformity with the laws of their nature, must of necessity, at all times, think and act rationally, unless they shall become physically, intellectually or morally diseased; in which case the council shall remove them into the hospital for bodily, mental, or moral invalids, where they shall remain until they shall have been recovered by the mildest treatment that can effect their cure.[22]

New Harmony did not last long enough for such treatment centers to be established. Not surprisingly (though it surprised Owen), other members of the community had different ideas about how life ought to be lived. Within a year a breakaway group established an alternative utopia two miles down the road. Then another group split off

---

[21]Robert Owen, *A New View of Society* (1813; London: J. M. Dent & Sons, 1927), pp. 16, 34.

[22]Robert Owen, *The Revolution in the Mind and Practice of the Human Race: Or, the Coming Change from Irrationality to Rationality* (London: J. M. Dent & Sons, 1849), p. 67.

and, in less than three years from the time it started, the attempt to establish a rationally grounded, scientific society collapsed completely. Owen sold the land and returned to England.

The ideas used by Mann to justify authoritarian control over children come from precisely the same source as the ideas we have been describing. Mann's view was that total control over children was justified by the fact that children's moral and intellectual development was governed by scientific laws, laws that could be systematically applied in school. As his biographer Jonathan Messerli put it, Mann thought that "by carefully identifying the input and rigorously controlling the process, the desired output was as clearly ordained as any scientific experiment or well-engineered industrial process."[23]

That again was illusory. Mann had no more scientific knowledge of the mind than had his educational predecessors. Instead of science, what one finds, as with Saint-Simon, Comte, and Owen, is pseudoscience coupled with an authoritarian moralizing by someone convinced that he has discerned what everyone else ought to know and how everyone else ought to live.

It is understandable that contemporary educators praise Mann for the "modernism" of his views. His conception of schooling is the one still being advanced today. Educators continue to claim scientific authority for their various programs and curricula. If anything, the demands for control have become more extreme.

It is suggested, for example, in an article in *Today's Education,* an official journal of the National Education Association, that teachers should be called "learning clinicians." That title, the authors say, "is intended to convey the idea that schools are becoming 'clinics' whose purpose is to provide individualized psychosocial 'treatment' for the students."[24] Here is one such plan for psychosocial treatment, proposed by James E. Allen Jr., at the time U.S. commissioner of education:

> Under the plan, there would be available in the school district a Central Diagnostic Center to which, at age 2½, a child would be brought by his parents or guardian. The

[23]Jonathan Messerli, *Horace Mann: A Biography* (New York: Alfred A. Knopf, 1972), p. 442.

[24]Harold Shane and June Shane, "Forecast for the '70s," *Today's Education,* January 1969, quoted in Peter Schrag and Diane Divoky, *The Myth of the Hyperactive Child* (New York: Pantheon Books, 1975), p. 19.

purpose of the Center would be to find out everything possible about the child and his background that would be useful in planning an individualized learning program for him. This would be accomplished through an educational diagnosis, a medical diagnosis, and home visits by a trained professional who would in effect become the child's and family's counselor. By the time the tests and home visits would be complete, the Center would know just about everything there is to know about this child—his home and family background, his cultural and language deficiencies, his health and nutrition needs, and his general potential as an individual.[25]

Although that plan was never adopted, it shows how outlandish the pseudoscientific authoritarianism of educational theory had become. Neither Commissioner Allen nor the authors of the NEA journal article point to any confirmed scientific theory on which their "treatments" might be based. And they could not, for there is no such theory.

Calling teachers "learning clinicians" is an abuse of language for the purpose of claiming the right to control and shape children, to subject them to "treatment." The title is intended to imply that there is some science, an educational science, that is being used in the process of formal schooling. But the idea that educators possess a scientifically grounded technology—for shaping orderly minds or rational problem solvers or worthy human beings—is, as it has always been, a myth. Noam Chomsky writes, in a survey of the field, "There exists no behavioral science incorporating nontrivial, empirically supported propositions that apply to human affairs or support a behavioral technology."[26]

What one finds in the schools is, not scientifically justified activities, but an assortment of tasks based on various educators' subjective views of what knowledge is "worthwhile" (Bruner) or "nutritious" (Van Doren) or "civilizing" (Boyer). Those views are then transformed into scientific truths by labeling them as such. And, finally, the claim is made that children are being shaped, for their

[25]Ibid., p. 6.

[26]Noam Chomsky, "Psychology and Ideology," in *For Reasons of State* (New York: Pantheon Books, 1973), p. 363.

93

own good, by a process that has been shown scientifically to be indispensable for proper mental development. In every one of its guises, that claim—and the authoritarian treatment of children based on it—is false.

8. Education and Individual Choice

What can be done? Are there changes that would improve the school system? Before attempting an answer, it is useful to consider why the system resists change when, even by its own standards, it is constantly failing.

The explanation, as many observers have pointed out, is that the school system is a bureaucratic monopoly, displaying the rigid, lethargic ineptitude that is characteristic of such enterprises in general. Economist James D. Gwartney writes,

> Why are our schools failing? Economic analysis indicates that they are failing for the same reasons that the socialist economies of Eastern Europe and the Soviet Union are failing. When production is regulated by politicians (and bureaucrats) rather than by competition for consumers, producers will spend more time catering to political officials and less time satisfying their customers. Since consumers are unable to shift their business to producers who provide them with "value for the price," suppliers have little incentive to produce efficiently, to innovate, or to figure out better ways of doing things. Simultaneously, since producers are operating in a noncompetitive environment, high costs and a poor-quality product (or service) do not lead to the loss of customers. Inefficient suppliers continue to survive and drain the resources of the economy.[1]

David Boaz of Washington's Cato Institute says,

> The government schools have failed because they are socialist institutions. Like Soviet factories, they are technologically backward, overstaffed, inflexible, unresponsive to consumer demand, and operated for the convenience of top-level bureaucrats. With every passing year, as we move further into the information age and the global economy, they

[1]James D. Gwartney, "How to Help Low-Income Students," in *Liberating Schools: Education in the Inner City*, ed. David Boaz (Washington: Cato Institute, 1991), p. 199.

become more inadequate. They are incapable of keeping up
with the needs of a dynamic and diverse society.[2]

The same insight comes from an unlikely source, Albert Shanker,
president of the American Federation of Teachers. "It's time to
admit," he writes,

> that public education operates like a planned economy, a
> bureaucratic system in which everybody's role is spelled out
> in advance and there are few incentives for innovation and
> productivity. It's no surprise that our school system doesn't
> improve: It more resembles the communist economy than
> our own market economy.[3]

There have been calls for change from within the educational
establishment itself, but those have consisted, for the most part, of
educators' exhorting each other to do better. "The public schools
have to become committed to excellence," says Bill Honig, former
California state superintendent of public instruction.[4] "The quality
of our schools must go up," says Ernest Boyer, president of the
Carnegie Foundation for the Advancement of Teaching.[5] But those
repeated appeals are largely ineffectual, and things remain essentially as they have always been. Since there is so little incentive to
improve, innovation is resisted at every level of the system. Even
such a relatively simple change as the introduction of a new textbook
is almost certain to encounter determined resistance. Teachers will
oppose it. And it is understandable that they will. They have become
accustomed to the old text, and they are not given any inducement
to make the extra effort to learn the new one.

Indeed, there is little motivation for teachers to make any extra
effort, to improve their teaching skills, to learn new methods of
instruction, to spend more time with a child who needs help. There
is no reward for superior performance. Nor is there any penalty for
incompetence. "The problem in the present regime," writes one
observer, "is that performance remains virtually irrelevant to teacher

[2]David Boaz, "The Public School Monopoly: America's Berlin Wall," in ibid., p. 21.
[3]Quoted in Boaz, p. 2.
[4]Bill Honig, *Last Chance for Our Children* (Menlo Park, Calif.: Addison-Wesley, 1985),
p. 28.
[5]Ernest L. Boyer, *High School* (New York: Harper & Row, 1983), p. 39.

security and advancement."[6] "Salary schedules," Milton Friedman points out, "tend to be uniform and determined far more by seniority, degrees received, and teaching certificates acquired than by merit."[7] Some teachers, of course, are motivated by idealism, and they try harder for that reason. But they are a minority.

There are many other sources of inefficiency. To mention just one, school districts are under constant pressure to spend all the money that has been allocated to them. If they don't, it will go into the general fund or to another, less efficient, district. Further, if a school district showed a surplus, "the excess funds might be subtracted from its allocation for the following year. . . . This common policy constitutes a strong deterrent against efficiency."[8]

In short, the bureaucratic, monopolistic structure of the school system and the practices that have resulted guarantee poor performance. If history has shown anything, it is that systems of that kind don't work. That is why the school system displays "all the energy and creativity of Soviet agriculture."[9]

The first step toward improvement is to end the government monopoly in education, to introduce competition into the field. Ted Kolderie, director of the Hubert H. Humphrey Institute of Public Affairs, puts the point precisely. The basic question, he says, is not how to improve the present educational system; it is how to create a system that seeks improvement.[10] What that requires is adopting a proposal made by John Stuart Mill almost 150 years ago, which has only recently begun to receive the attention it deserves:

> If the government would make up its mind to require for every child a good education, it might save itself the trouble of providing one. It might leave to parents to obtain the education where and how they pleased, and content itself with helping to pay the school fees of the poorer classes of children, and defraying the entire school expenses of those

[6]John E. Coons, "Perestroika and the Private Provider," in *Liberating Schools*, p. 185.

[7]Milton Friedman, *Capitalism and Freedom* (Chicago: University of Chicago Press, 1962), p. 95.

[8]Myron Lieberman, *Privatization and Educational Choice* (New York: St. Martin's, 1989), p. 45.

[9]Boaz, p. 14.

[10]Ted Kolderie, "Education That Works: The Right Role for Business," *Harvard Business Review* 5 (September–October 1987): 56–62.

who have no one else to pay for them. . . . An education established and controlled by the State should only exist, if it exist at all, as one among many competing experiments.[11]

School Vouchers

The change to a competitive system would not be difficult to bring about. There are numerous proposals already available for funding a system of parental choice. Perhaps the best known is Milton Friedman's voucher plan. Under that plan, parents of schoolchildren would receive an educational voucher from the government for an amount equal to the per capita expenditure on public schooling. The parents would then be free to use the voucher to pay for their child's education at a school of their choice, public or private. Many other funding possibilities are discussed in detail in Myron Lieberman's *Privatization and Educational Choice*. What all of those proposals have in common is that they seek to replace the present system with one in which children and their parents have a choice among competing schools.

The advantages of a system of educational choice are many. The most obvious is that an arrangement is created in which the providers of educational services, the schools, do have an interest in efficiency and improved performance. Instead of a stagnant, monopolistic structure that prevents others from trying to do better, there is a competitive environment that invites and encourages innovation.

Another advantage of that system is that it gives to all parents an opportunity now open only to a few, the opportunity to select a school appropriate for their child. Pete du Pont, former governor of Delaware and chairman of the Education Commission of the States, writes,

> My wife, Elise, and I have four children. They're all different, and they all had different educational needs. One is very bright and needed a rigorous academic environment. Another is dyslexic and needed a very special school. Another is scientifically inclined, the other more artistic; they needed schools that would suit them. Fortunately, Elise and I could afford to choose the school best suited to each of our children. All parents should have that opportunity. One

[11]John Stuart Mill, *On Liberty* (1859; New York: Bobbs-Merrill, 1956), p. 129.

cannot treat all children the same way because every child is different.[12]

The opportunity to choose among schools yields the most important advantage of a competitive system: it introduces into the field of education a responsiveness to the consumer, the family. As things stand now, parents who are dissatisfied with a school policy are virtually powerless. When they try to act on behalf of their children against a school policy, they are regarded as a nuisance. Consider a problem involving a conflict between parents and a school. Suppose that the child, like one of Governor du Pont's children, is scientifically inclined. Because he is not artistically inclined, he doesn't like his art class. He's carving a head of Geronimo. But it doesn't look like anything. He can't get it to look like anything—and he doesn't want to. He would just like to stop doing it and continue his investigation of paramecia, blood worms, frogs, fruit flies, rock formations, and constellations.

Imagine that the parents come to school to request that the child be transferred to a different class where he would be more involved. They will not have much chance of success. The principal, or more likely some deputy, will say, "That's not a valid reason." And that will be the end of it. Maybe, if they are especially courageous, the parents will persist a bit longer: "But Edward doesn't like to whittle. Neither of us likes to whittle, for that matter. No one in our whole family is much of a whittler. Why should Edward have to do it? Forcing him to do something he finds so dull, day after day, does not seem to us to be a thoughtful way of dealing with a child." That too will have little effect. The school will say, "We don't give special treatment" or "This is not a department store."

If a school in a competitive atmosphere were to respond that way, the parents could take the child elsewhere. They would not have to accept such insensitive, peremptory treatment. Because they would have options, the parents would be in a position to insist that Edward's character, interests, and needs be taken into account. They could decide that his being bored counted against the school. In the present system, the school counts it against Edward.

[12]Pete du Pont, "Education Enterprise Zones," in *Liberating Schools*, p. 208.

In contrast to the situation in which schools can dismiss parents' ideas out of hand, competition will result in schools that are required, for their own survival, to be sensitive and responsive to that kind of parental concern. The result will be that greater attention is given to the individuality of children. The school system will begin to address the fact that different children have different needs.

Defenders of the present system have challenged the idea of privatizing schools on a number of grounds. The most frequently encountered argument is that a system of competing schools, financed by the government, would violate the constitutional principle of the separation of church and state. It is held that, since some parents would use the vouchers to send their children to parochial schools, the government would, in effect, be subsidizing religion.

But that objection does not have much weight. In the first place, there is no more reason for saying that the government would be subsidizing religion in this case than there is for saying it is subsidizing religion when it gives a welfare check to someone who uses part of the money to make a church contribution. The government would be subsidizing the education of children, some of whose parents would want that education to be in a sectarian institution.

In the second place, a voucher system has already existed, without being seen as a violation of the separation of church and state. At the end of World War II, under the terms of the GI Bill, returning veterans were given money by the government to pay for their college education. That was done whether or not the recipient chose a church-related institution, as many did. Indeed, the GI Bill is the model Friedman refers to in explaining his voucher plan. The same principle is involved in both.

Some critics have objected on the grounds that a choice system might result in less freedom than there is at present. It might happen that schools that are now relatively free of government interference would, in the new system, find themselves more regulated, more regimented. Since the government would be involved in funding the system, it would have to establish criteria for what constitutes a school. That opens the possibility that all schools, including the private ones, would be forced to adopt exactly the same practices as the public ones. Boaz comments,

> Through the regulatory process, state governments could turn independent schools into perfect copies of the government schools—burdened by paperwork, hamstrung by

bureaucracy, top-heavy with administrative personnel and guideline writers. The government would have surreptitiously destroyed the existing alternatives to the public school monopoly.[13]

The point, I think, is well taken. There is no human institution that cannot be corrupted. And it might happen that competition would be introduced in name only. Not only might it happen, there will be pressure for it to happen. Government regulators, when given the chance, tend to regulate as much as possible. But it will also be apparent to people that there is a connection, an inverse relationship, between the degree of governmental control and the range of their choices. So some parents will be exerting a counterpressure to governmental attempts to impose uniformity. As they come to see the value of competition, more people will demand the same variety of choices with respect to the education of their children that they are accustomed to in other areas of their lives.

The fundamental objection to a choice system is to the idea of parental choice itself. The schools, it is held, should not be responsive to parents in the way proposed. Parents shouldn't be able to tell a school what class a child should or shouldn't be in. Parents are not in a position to decide whether what the school is doing is worthwhile. They are not experts. The education of a child is a matter for educational professionals. An English educator writes, in opposition to parental choice,

> I'm not sure that parents know what is best educationally for their children. They know what's best for them to eat. They know the best environment they can provide at home. But we've been trained to ascertain the problems of children, to detect their weaknesses, to put right those things that need putting right, and we want to do this freely, with the cooperation of parents and not under undue strains.[14]

The assertion that the experts, trained in educational science, know how to "put things right" or how to prevent a child's having "a lopsided mind" is supposed to convince us that parents should not

[13]Boaz, p. 26.

[14]Quoted in Milton Friedman and Rose Friedman, *Free to Choose* (New York: Avon Books, 1981), p. 174.

be making educational decisions. Parents are no more in a position to question the judgment of educators than they are in a position to question the judgment of a brain surgeon.

That view, which sees schooling as the giving of psychosocial treatment, or as the scientific shaping of the mind and character of a child, is the view we have been examining throughout the present work. Parents are not simply sending their children to school to be taught. They are turning their children over to school to be constructed. As Horace Mann put it, "We who are engaged in the sacred cause of education are entitled to look upon all parents as having given hostages to our cause."[15]

As we have seen, educators' claims to scientific knowledge have no foundation. There is no such thing as educational science. Those who have wanted to control the lives of others have always claimed to know exactly what others need. They have always believed that their plans represent order, as opposed to the chaos that would ensue without them. When Robert Owen defended imposing his way of thinking on the members of New Harmony, he claimed that the issue was

> whether the character of man shall continue to be formed under the guidance of the most inconsistent notions, the errors of which for centuries past have been manifest to every reflecting rational mind; or whether it shall be moulded under the direction of uniformly consistent principles, derived from the unvarying facts of the creation.[16]

The trouble with all such views is that their authors are deluded in thinking that their plans are "derived from the unvarying facts of the creation." "I have discovered what everyone needs," each one says. "My superior insight" (Mann) or "my divine foresight" (Saint-Simon) or "my research in the field" (Watson, Skinner, Piaget, and countless others) "has enabled me to ascertain what human beings require if they are to become rational, enlightened, civilized, autonomous." Every one of those mind-designing schemes, however, when looked at closely, has turned out to have little to do with

[15]Horace Mann, *Lectures and Annual Reports on Education,* ed. Mary Mann (Cambridge, Mass.: Published for the editor, 1867), p. 184.

[16]Robert Owen, *A New View of Society* (1813; London: J. M. Dent & Sons, 1927), pp. 46–47.

either science or order. What one finds is pure subjectivity offered as science and arbitrariness disguised as order.

The result is that schools have been imposing on children just the opposite of what the professional educators claim. According to the rhetoric, schools follow an ordered plan, constructed by experts, based on a scientific understanding of mental development. But even the most casual look at what the school system actually offers shows that there is no ordered plan at all. David and Micki Colfax write,

> The public school curriculum—which embodies, at least theoretically, what is to be learned and when—is in fact nothing more than a hodgepodge of materials and assumptions resulting from the historical interplay of educational theories, political expedience, education fads and fashions, pretensions to culture, demagoguery, and demography. It is by no means, as the professional educators would have it, a coherent "course of study" or, as the more pretentious among them would have it, a "distillation of our common culture."[17]

That is a kind way of putting the point. In actuality, there is no public school curriculum. Every state, every county, every educational committee has its own idea of how to shape people and form their character. Every educational theorist has his or her particular notion of what constitutes indispensable human knowledge. Professor Bruner thinks it necessary for children to acquire the "self-conscious understanding of the linguist." Another educator declares that children have to learn set theory "if they are to make any intelligent adjustment whatsoever to modern life."[18] Mortimer Adler and his Paideia Group insist that every child be taught to play the recorder and to "make simple, useful objects from wood and other common materials."[19] The state of Wisconsin says that no education is complete without a thorough understanding of "the food and

[17]David Colfax and Micki Colfax, *Homeschooling for Excellence* (New York: Warner Books, 1988), p. 39.

[18]Lawrence A. Cremin, *The Genius of American Education* (New York: Vintage Books, 1965), p. 59.

[19]Mortimer Adler, ed., *The Paideia Program* (New York: Macmillan, 1984), pp. 147, 155.

health values of dairy products and their importance for human diet."[20]

But even if educational theory were not riddled with ridiculous pretension, it would still be a mistake to try to impose a blueprint for mental development on everyone. To do so is to ignore the truth of Governor du Pont's observation that children all have different needs. It is to ignore the character and interests of the individual child and to impose on every child something that is arbitrary, artificial, limited, and limiting.

John Stuart Mill wrote,

> There is no reason that all human existence should be constructed on some one or some small number of patterns. . . . Human beings are not like sheep; and even sheep are not indistinguishably alike. . . . If it were only that people have diversities of taste, that is reason enough for not attempting to shape them all after one model. . . . The same things which are helps to one person toward the cultivation of his higher nature are hindrances to another. The same mode of life is a healthy excitement to one, keeping all his faculties of action and enjoyment in their best order, while to another it is a distracting burden which suspends or crushes all internal life. Such are the differences among human beings in their sources of pleasure, their susceptibilities of pain, and the operation on them of different physical and moral agencies that, unless there is a corresponding diversity in their modes of life, they neither obtain their fair share of happiness, nor grow up to the mental, moral, and aesthetic stature of which their nature is capable.[21]

Individuality

Here one comes to the heart of the matter. The public school system, despite occasional lip service to the idea, has been at war with individuality. It forces its developmental plans on every child in the false belief that they express general scientific truths. It has done so from its inception. Mann's central premise, writes his biographer Jonathan Messerli, was that since "all children everywhere

[20]Boyer, p. 59.
[21]Mill, p. 83.

104

were essentially the same, all could be taught, once the correct techniques and goals were determined."[22] The idea was that "a system of instruction which would work for some, would work for all."[23] One of Mann's colleagues, Solomon Adams, expressed the view this way:

> If a well-conducted education produces benevolence, justice, truth, patriotism, love to God, and love to man, in one case, the same education, in the same circumstances, will produce the same results in all cases.[24]

Even if the methods were scientific, it would not follow that all children should travel the same path. Only if children were as similar as hydrogen atoms would the "circumstances" be the same. But they are not. The essence of the process of human development is individuation and self-differentiation. Nothing is of greater importance to a growing child, write psychiatrists Stella Chess and Alexander Thomas, than "self-discovery, self-awareness, self-realization, self-fulfillment."[25] Psychologist Abraham Maslow writes that the "natural inclinations, propensities or inner bent constitute the 'inner core' of a human being."[26] One damages a child, he says, when one suppresses that inner core. Individual development is not encouraged by imposing the same set of interests and activities on every child. On the contrary, writes child psychologist Kay McDonald, "The first guideline for enhancing positive self-concepts is to recognize, respect, and encourage individual differences."[27]

The contrast between that way of thinking about children and that of most educators could not be greater. Educators, in the belief that they have scientific knowledge of what everyone needs, see

[22]Jonathan Messerli, *Horace Mann: A Biography* (New York: Alfred A. Knopf, 1972), p. 443.

[23]Ibid., p. 444.

[24]Quoted in ibid.

[25]Stella Chess and Alexander Thomas, *The Dynamics of Psychological Development* (New York: Brunner/Mazel, 1980), p. 195.

[26]Abraham H. Maslow, *Toward a Psychology of Being* (New York: Van Nostrand Reinhold, 1968), p. 193.

[27]Kay A. McDonald, "Enhancing a Child's Positive Self-Concept," in *The Self-Concept of the Young Child*, ed. Thomas D. Yawkey (Provo, Utah: Brigham Young University Press, 1980), p. 54.

themselves as justified in ignoring the character and interests of the individual children they are shaping. Robert Hutchins, former president of the University of Chicago and cofounder (with Mortimer Adler) of the Great Books Program, puts the point bluntly. According to Hutchins, the child's perception of the tasks required by school is "irrelevant."[28]

In the same spirit, Professor Bruner ignored the negative reactions to his teaching. He described how, in his MACOS class, the children actually groaned at the repetitive tedium of his lessons. A girl called out, in a burst of agonized wit, "Are we going to distribute the Distributive Law again?"[29] But Bruner paid no attention to her and went on with his lesson. It was as though she hadn't spoken. Why? Because he deceived himself into believing that what he was doing was justified by science. He was scientifically managing the mental development of the children so that their minds would not be lopsided. Given the importance of that mission, the girl's objection was no more to be heeded than would be a child's objection to being vaccinated. But that is a false analogy. What Bruner was doing had no scientific foundation, in learning theory or any other theory. His justification for insisting that children study the fundamentals of modern linguistics was that he and some of his colleagues decided that they were "worth an adult's knowing." That approach produced the opposite of what was intended, not a self-confident, searching mind, but bewilderment and boredom and alienated anger.

With competing schools there will not be such casual suppression of the character and interests of children in favor of some expert's personal taste. As schools pay more attention to the individuality of children, they will begin to help children develop a greater sense of what their interests and inclinations are. Instead of having them memorize meaningless dates and mechanically mouth formulas, the tendency will be for children to be engaged in activities in which they are genuinely interested. And then schools will become places that encourage meaningful learning. Meaningful learning, Paul

[28]Quoted in Sol Cohen, ed., *Education in the United States: A Documentary History* (New York: Random House, 1974), p. 2799.

[29]Jerome Bruner, *Toward a Theory of Instruction* (New York: W. W. Norton, 1966), p. 69.

Goodman points out, cannot come about unless there is genuine involvement.

> Nothing can be efficiently learned, or, indeed learned at all—other than through parroting or brute training, when acquired knowledge is promptly forgotten after the examination—unless it meets need, desire, curiosity, or fantasy. Unless there is a reaching from within, the learning cannot become "second nature," as Aristotle called true learning.[30]

Would instituting a system of educational choice address the problems of the arbitrary and authoritarian practices of the present school system? Privately operated schools, after all, have not up to now been especially sensitive to the individuality of their students. Indeed, in many cases, such as in religious and military schools, they have been more authoritarian and restrictive than the public schools. But that fact can be misleading. Those who establish or send their children to private schools generally do so because they have a particular agenda. They have the strong belief that children should be molded and shaped. Discipline and obedience tend to be paramount values and, more often than not, children are sent to schools of that sort to learn to toe the line.

In an atmosphere of free competition, no doubt, such schools will continue to exist. But there will be other schools that are genuinely responsive to children's interests, and concerned about encouraging them. Those schools will reflect the increasing respect for children as individuals that has been emerging in recent years. One sees that changing attitude in, for example, the formation of numerous organizations concerned with defending children's rights and in such legal advances as the Supreme Court's landmark *In re Gault* decision, granting children tried in juvenile court the right to counsel and to confront and cross-examine their accusers.

But it might seem that even if there is a tendency toward more individualistic treatment, the differences between the new schools and the old will not be great. Much of the character of schooling is determined by what the curriculum is, by what standards the children have to satisfy. And even supporters of educational choice have not questioned traditional school standards in any serious way.

---

[30]Paul Goodman, "No Processing Whatever," in *Radical School Reform*, ed. Ronald Gross and Beatrice Gross (New York: Simon and Schuster, 1969), p. 99.

In fact, their support for educational choice is based on the belief that it will result in schools better able to prepare children to meet those standards. Their disagreements with the present system generally focus on the methods, not the matter, of schooling.

However, in a self-examining system, unlike the present one, there is no doubt that the question of what should be taught will be examined as well as the question of how it is to be taught. For example, if it is really true that children are studying algebra so that their powers of logical thought will be strengthened, or so that they will be better able to solve the problems of life after having solved so many algebra problems, then there is no justification for algebra. It is impossible to predict in any detail exactly what direction the process of self-examination will take. And so it is impossible to predict in detail how schools will change. But one thing is sure: a system of competing schools will produce a vigorous and thorough discussion of standards, and there is not even a remote chance of that happening in the present system.

One might think that if the questioning of school standards is desirable, then giving more power to parents is not what is needed. Most parents believe in the standards of the schools. If anything, they are more extreme in their demands—they want more mathematics, more book reports, more homework.

It is true that most parents, like most people in general, support the demands made on children by the schools. That is not surprising. From an early age, everyone is told, directly or indirectly, in innumerable ways, that the degree to which a person meets school standards is an accurate measure of that person's mental ability. The widespread acceptance of that notion makes it clear that significant change will not occur overnight. Were a system of competing schools to be adopted, most schools would not, at the outset, be very different from those of today. One could well expect that they would require children to memorize formulas and pile up information.

However, there are observers of children, though they still constitute a minority, who have insisted on the necessity of paying greater attention to the individual differences among children. And it is not just psychologists studying childhood, such as Eda LeShan and Abraham Maslow, who have come to that conclusion. Some parents have had that insight as well. Their different approach to children is perhaps seen most clearly in some of the parents who have rejected the traditional educational system and opted for homeschooling.

David and Micki Colfax, in *Homeschooling for Excellence*, describe how they gradually became aware, as many parents do, that their children were being badly affected by schooling. Children who had been active and voluble became withdrawn and listless when school was in session. But unlike the majority of parents, who tend to blame the problem on the child, they went to observe what was going on. What struck them most about what they saw was that in school the individual interests of their children were "of no consequence." The children were "expected, compelled, usually for not very good reasons, to respond to the dictates of others." The day was filled with "pointless and time-consuming assignments." To the children it was "dumb" and "a waste of time."[31] In this case, unlike most, the parents agreed.

The Colfaxes withdrew their children from school. Apart from some legally mandated concessions to the school curriculum, the children were encouraged to follow their interests. Naturally, the paths they took diverged. They became interested in different things, in different ways. One child learned to read at four, another not until he was nine, when "his desire to know about the Pomo Indians who once camped on our ridge required that he learn to read."[32] One child was writing short stories before he was 10, while another wrote very little "until he began doing a weekly column on astronomy for the local newspaper."[33]

The fact that three of their four children wound up at Harvard University led to the Colfaxes' receiving a great deal of praise. But that academic result, as they are aware, is not what marks their success as parents. Their success is evident in the healthy, vital, self-confident spirits of their children, children who were spared the generalizing misdirection of the typical school.

Of course, not everyone can do what the Colfaxes did. Many parents, even those who would want their children to get the benefits of a program tailored to their individual strengths and interests, do not have the time or the inclination or the patience of the Colfaxes. So there will be schools answering to that desire. Schools will not only compete with respect to efficiency. There will also be competing

[31]Colfax and Colfax, pp. 28, 21.
[32]Ibid., p. 55.
[33]Ibid., p. 75.

visions of children. Since the recognition of children's individuality is of fundamental importance in encouraging mental growth and general self-confidence, the advantages for children of schooling that manifests that attitude will, over time, become evident. What the Colfaxes discovered first-hand is this: if children are allowed to pursue what interests, fascinates, and intrigues them, are allowed to try things out according to their own lights, are not constantly acting out of fear of making mistakes and so are able to learn from mistakes, then the process of mental growth will be richer and healthier than what issues from some supposedly universally applicable curriculum for "proper" human mental development.

When one looks closely at the ideas of educators, it seems remarkable that their claims to scientific knowledge and the right to control the development of children still enjoy such wide acceptance. We have seen only a few examples of the false, and even outlandish, notions educators have embraced: "A few hundred pages of information separate dependence from autonomy"; "learning to solve problems in algebra will equip one with the ability to handle the problem-solving situation"; "knowledge of the fundamentals of linguistics is necessary if one is to avoid having a lopsided mind." Those are fitting companions for Mann's declaration that crime can be prevented by "a degree of common knowledge easily taught and common honesty to which all children with scarcely an exception might be trained."[34]

What has resulted from insights like those is a form of life that is, as *Fortune* editor Charles Silberman rightly says, intellectually and aesthetically barren. It is an environment in which children are controlled by random demands that, for the most part, serve no purpose but to distort self-expression and self-awareness.

If one follows the trail of those insights and looks at their actual, real-world consequences, as opposed to the educators' fantasies, one cannot avoid seeing the pain and suppression they produce. Eda LeShan, in *The Conspiracy against Childhood*, tells of the case of Charles who, at 16, had failed math and French. Consequently, he had to go to summer school instead of doing what he had intended, serving as a volunteer recreation leader at a work camp in Appalachia. His mother said, "It really serves him right—maybe this will teach him

[34]Mann, p. 237.

a lesson." Charles's parents, viewing him in terms of the standards imposed by school, considered him lazy, detached, and irresponsible. The truth was quite different.

> What was Charles really like? It is true that he had great difficulty driving himself to do things that did not interest him. In addition, however, he had a marvelous wry wit, a delicious sense of humor, and a truly creative and imaginative mind for those things that intrigued him. He had many close friends; he could be counted on to help them in any rough situation. Three years before, he had taught himself to play the guitar, and at fifteen he was so good that he had been asked to be the guitar instructor at a sophisticated music camp with very high standards. He had worked at another camp the summer before—a drama camp, in which he took part in a different play every week. No job was too menial or dirty, and he had somehow managed to take additional courses offered in art. This experience had started him off on a new interest, and he wanted very much to take an intensive course in art history at a nearby college while still attending high school, but this plan had been forbidden because of his failing work in math and French.[35]

One sees here, in a concrete case, the damage to a person caused by the false tasks imposed by educators. There is benevolence in Charles, and creativity and generosity and courage and dedication. Those are valuable human characteristics, and they constitute the essence of Charles. They are what is best in him. It is a mistake to shut them down. But that is exactly what is happening. They are being suppressed, and for no good reason. Charles is being deprived of the opportunity to express and cultivate those qualities so that he can learn to master "the problem-solving process" by working on exercises in algebra. What takes place in his life is being determined, not by his ardent and benevolent desires, not by what his spirit craves, but by a casually tossed off, nebulous thought about problem solving, a thought that has nothing to do with him and little to do with problem solving. He is being directed by a plan that was arrived at entirely independent of any knowledge of him and that, consequently, takes no notice of his character, of his needs,

---

[35]Eda LeShan, *The Conspiracy against Childhood* (New York: Atheneum, 1980), p. 257.

of what is special or different about him. What are the chances that such a plan is going to be helpful to him, a unique individual?

Educators blame the children for rejecting their offerings. They say that the children are lazy or lacking in curiosity or resistant to learning. It was not a lack of curiosity that caused Einstein to experience his own schooling as "the negation of the human being."[36] Nor is laziness the reason Woody Allen thanks God every morning that he doesn't have to go to school. Here is where one should locate the failure of schooling as it has existed up to now, in its producing those reactions, not only in Einstein and Woody Allen, but in millions of other, less illustrious, but no less humanly worthwhile, people. After all, what is the explanation of those reactions? It is that the human spirit does not thrive on arbitrary restraint, that it doesn't flourish in an atmosphere that constantly substitutes generalized rules for individual goals. Individualism, wrote Oscar Wilde,

> comes naturally and inevitably out of man. It is the point to which all development tends. It is the differentiation to which all organisms grow. It is the perfection that is inherent in every mode of life, and towards which every mode of life quickens. To ask whether individualism is practical is like asking whether evolution is practical. Evolution is the law of life, and there is no evolution except towards individualism. When this tendency is not expressed, it is a case of artificially arrested growth, or of disease, or of death.[37]

Could it really be true that the public school system is the best that adults have to offer children? What is certain is that as long as the monopoly is perpetuated, it will never get any better. But a system in which competition fuels innovation will get better. It will lead, writes Boaz, "to the selection of the best ideas for educational improvement—not just those currently being tried by government schools but also new ideas that bureaucrats would never dream of and that entrepreneurs will naturally discover."[38]

---

[36]Ronald W. Clark, *Einstein: The Life and Times* (New York: World Publishing, 1971), p. 14.

[37]Oscar Wilde, *The Soul of Man under Socialism*, in *The Works of Oscar Wilde* (New York: P. F. Collier & Son, 1927), p. 510.

[38]Boaz, p. 49.

It is time to create an environment in which schools will not only operate efficiently but will also, more important, recognize and respond to the fact that children are all different and have different needs. It is time to create an environment that will nurture and encourage individuality instead of treating it as irrelevant. The means for inaugurating such a change are at hand.

Selected Bibliography

Adler, Mortimer, ed. *The Paideia Program*. New York: Macmillan, 1984.

Barker, Stephen F. "Geometry." In *The Encyclopedia of Philosophy*. Edited by Paul Edwards. New York: Free Press, 1967.

Beberman, Max. "An Emerging Program of Secondary School Mathematics." In *Education in the United States: A Documentary History*. Edited by Sol Cohen. New York: Random House, 1974.

Berlin, Isaiah. *Against the Current*. Harmondsworth, U.K.: Penguin Books, 1979.

Bestor, Arthur. *Educational Wastelands*. Urbana and Chicago: University of Illinois Press, 1953.

Boaz, David. "The Public School Monopoly: America's Berlin Wall." In *Liberating Schools: Education in the Inner City*. Edited by David Boaz. Washington: Cato Institute, 1991.

Boaz, David, ed. *Liberating Schools: Education in the Inner City*. Washington: Cato Institute, 1991.

Boole, George. *Collected Logical Works*. Chicago: Open Court, 1940.

Boyer, Ernest L. *High School*. New York: Harper & Row, 1983.

Brainerd, Charles J. *Piaget's Theory of Intelligence*. Englewood Cliffs, N.J.: Prentice-Hall, 1978.

Brecht, Arnold. *The Political Education of Arnold Brecht: An Autobiography, 1884–1970*. Princeton, N.J.: Princeton University Press, 1970.

Bregman, E. O. "An Attempt to Modify the Emotional Attitudes of Children by the Conditioned Response Technique." *Journal of Genetic Psychology* 45 (1934): 169–98.

Breland, Keller, and Marian Breland. "The Misbehavior of Organisms." In *Biological Boundaries of Learning*. Edited by Martin E. P. Seligman and Joanne L. Hager. New York: Appleton-Century-Crofts, 1972.

Broad, C. D. *The Mind and Its Place in Nature*. London: Routledge & Kegan Paul, 1925.

Bruner, Jerome. *The Process of Education*. Cambridge, Mass.: Harvard University Press, 1960.

———. *Toward a Theory of Instruction*. New York: W. W. Norton, 1966.

Buckley, Kerry W. *Mechanical Man: John Broadus Watson and the Beginnings of Behaviorism*. New York: Guilford, 1989.

Chess, Stella, and Alexander Thomas. *The Dynamics of Psychological Development*. New York: Brunner/Mazel, 1980.

Chomsky, Noam. "Psychology and Ideology." In *For Reasons of State*. New York: Pantheon Books, 1973.

————. "Recent Contributions to the Theory of Innate Ideas." In *The Philosophy of Language*. Edited by J. R. Searle. London: Oxford University Press, 1971.

————. "A Review of B. F. Skinner's *Verbal Behavior*." In *The Structure of Language: Readings in the Philosophy of Language*. Edited by Jerry A. Fodor and Jerrold J. Katz. Englewood Cliffs, N.J.: Prentice-Hall, 1964.

Clark, Ronald W. *Einstein: The Life and Times*. New York: World Publishing, 1971.

Cohen, David. *J. B. Watson: Founder of Behaviorism*. London: Routledge & Kegan Paul, 1979.

Cohen, Sol, ed. *Education in the United States: A Documentary History*. New York: Random House, 1974.

Colfax, David, and Micki Colfax. *Homeschooling for Excellence*. New York: Warner Books, 1988.

Conant, James B. *The American High School Today*. New York: Signet Books, 1959.

Coons, John E. "Perestroika and the Private Provider." In *Liberating Schools: Education in the Inner City*. Edited by David Boaz. Washington: Cato Institute, 1991.

Cremin, Lawrence A. *The Genius of American Education*. New York: Vintage Books, 1965.

————. "Horace Mann's Legacy." In *The Republic and the School*. Edited by Lawrence A. Cremin. New York: Teachers College, Columbia, 1957.

————. *The Transformation of the School*. New York: Vintage Books, 1964.

deMause, Lloyd. "The Evolution of Childhood." In *The History of Childhood*. Edited by Lloyd deMause. New York: Psychohistory Press, 1974.

Dennett, Daniel C. "Skinner Skinned." In *Brainstorms: Philosophical Essays on Mind and Psychology*. Cambridge, Mass.: Bradford Books, 1978.

Dewey, John. *John Dewey on Education*. Edited by Reginald D. Archambault. Chicago: University of Chicago Press, 1964.

du Pont, Pete. "Education Enterprise Zones." In *Liberating Schools: Education in the Inner City*. Edited by David Boaz. Washington: Cato Institute, 1991.

Einstein, Albert. *Ideas and Opinions*. New York: Bonanza Books, 1954.

Elkind, David. *Miseducation*. New York: Alfred A. Knopf, 1987.

Emerson, Ralph Waldo. "Education." In *The Portable Emerson*. Edited by Mark Van Doren. New York: Viking, 1946.

————. *English Traits*. New York: P. F. Collier & Son, 1909.

Fichte, Johann Gottlieb. *Addresses to the German Nation*. New York: Harper & Row, 1968.

Friedman, Milton. *Capitalism and Freedom*. Chicago: University of Chicago Press, 1962.

Friedman, Milton, and Rose Friedman. *Free to Choose*. New York: Avon Books, 1981.

Friedrich, Otto. *Glenn Gould*. New York: Vintage Books, 1989.

Gross, Ronald, and Beatrice Gross, eds. *Radical School Reform*. New York: Simon and Schuster, 1969.

Gwartney, James D. "How to Help Low-Income Students." In *Liberating Schools: Education in the Inner City*. Edited by David Boaz. Washington: Cato Institute, 1991.

Hartley, Mariette. *Breaking the Silence*. New York: Penguin Books, 1990.

Hayek, F. A. *The Counter-Revolution of Science*. Glencoe, Ill.: Free Press, 1952.

———. *New Studies in Philosophy, Politics, Economics and the History of Ideas*. London: Routledge & Kegan Paul, 1978.

Hirsch, E. D., Jr. *Cultural Literacy: What Every American Needs to Know*. Boston: Houghton Mifflin, 1987.

Hirsch, E. D., Jr., et al. *Dictionary of Cultural Literacy*. Boston: Houghton Mifflin, 1988.

Hofstadter, Richard. *Anti-Intellectualism in American Life*. New York: Alfred A. Knopf, 1963.

Holt, John. *The Underachieving School*. New York: Dell, 1972.

Honig, Bill. *Last Chance for Our Children*. Menlo Park, Calif.: Addison-Wesley, 1985.

Hull, Clark L. *Principles of Behavior*. New York: Appleton-Century-Crofts, 1943.

Illich, Ivan. *Deschooling Society*. New York: Harper & Row, 1971.

Illick, Joseph E. "Child-Rearing in Seventeenth-Century England and America." In *The History of Childhood*. Edited by Lloyd deMause. New York: Psychology Press, 1974.

Kline, Morris. *Mathematics: The Loss of Certainty*. Oxford: Oxford University Press, 1980.

———. *Why Johnny Can't Add: The Failure of the New Math*. New York: Vintage Books, 1974.

Kolderie, Ted. "Education That Works: The Right Role for Business." *Harvard Business Review* 5 (September-October 1987): 56–62.

Lang, Cecil Y., ed. *The Swinburne Letters*. New Haven, Conn.: Yale University Press, 1959.

Lebowitz, Fran. *Social Studies*. New York: Pocket Books, 1982.

Leibniz, Gottfried Wilhelm von. *Selections*. Edited by Philip P. Wiener. New York: Scribner, 1951.

LeShan, Eda J. *The Conspiracy against Childhood*. New York: Atheneum, 1980.

Lichtenberg, Georg Christoph. *Werke in Einem Band*. Hamburg: Hoffmann und Campe, 1967.

Lieberman, Myron. *Privatization and Educational Choice*. New York: St. Martin's, 1989.

Locke, John. *Some Thoughts Concerning Education*. In *On Politics and Education*. Edited by Howard R. Penniman. New York: D. Van Nostrand, 1947.

Mann, Horace. *Lectures and Annual Reports on Education*. Edited by Mary Mann. Cambridge, Mass.: Published for the editor, 1867.

Maslow, Abraham H. *Toward a Psychology of Being*. New York: Van Nostrand Reinhold, 1968.

Matthews, Gareth B. *Philosophy and the Young Child*. Cambridge, Mass.: Harvard University Press, 1980.

Mencken, H. L. *A Mencken Chrestomathy*. New York: Alfred A. Knopf, 1949.

Meredith, George. *Letters: Collected and Edited by His Son*. New York: Charles Scribner's Sons, 1912.

Messerli, Jonathan. *Horace Mann: A Biography*. New York: Alfred A. Knopf, 1972.

Mill, John Stuart. *On Liberty*. New York: Bobbs-Merrill, 1956.

Moore, Raymond S., and Dorothy N. Moore. *School Can Wait*. Provo, Utah: Brigham Young University Press, 1979.

Nietzsche, Friedrich. *Human, All-Too-Human*. New York: Russell & Russell, 1964.

———. *Twilight of the Idols*. In *The Portable Nietzsche*. Edited by Walter Kaufmann. New York: Viking Press, 1954.

Owen, Robert. *A New View of Society*. 1813. Reprint, London: J. M. Dent & Sons, 1927.

———. *The Revolution in the Mind and Practice of the Human Race: Or, the Coming Change from Irrationality to Rationality*. London: J. M. Dent & Sons, 1849.

Pascal, Blaise. *Pensées*. New York: E. P. Dutton, 1958.

Peters, R. S. *The Concept of Motivation*. London: Routledge & Kegan Paul, 1958.

Piaget, Jean. *Science of Education and the Psychology of the Child*. New York: Orion, 1970.

Pope, Alexander. *An Essay on Criticism*. Edited by E. Audra and Aubrey Williams. London: Methuen, 1961.

Ravitch, Diane. *The Troubled Crusade: American Education, 1945–1980*. New York: Basic Books, 1983.

Ravitch, Diane, and Chester Finn. *What Do Our 17-Year-Olds Know?* New York: Harper & Row, 1987.

Samuel, R. H., and R. Hinton Thomas. *Education and Society in Modern Germany*. London: Routledge & Kegan Paul, 1949.

Schrag, Peter, and Diane Divoky. *The Myth of the Hyperactive Child*. New York: Pantheon Books, 1975.

Seligman, Martin E. P. "On the Generality of the Laws of Learning." *Psychological Review* 77, no. 5 (1970): 406–18.

Silberman, Charles. *Crisis in the Classroom*. New York: Random House, 1970.

Skinner, B. F. *The Behavior of Organisms*. New York: Appleton-Century-Crofts, 1938.

Smith, Nila Banton. *Reading Instruction for Today's Children*. Englewood Cliffs, N.J.: Prentice-Hall, 1963.

Stevenson, Robert Louis. "Henry David Thoreau: His Character and Opinions." In *Familiar Studies of Men and Books*. New York: Charles Scribner's Sons, 1907.

Still, G. F. *The History of Pediatrics*. London: Oxford University Press, 1931.

Strawson, P. F. *Introduction to Logical Theory*. London: Methuen, 1952.

Tchaikovsky, Modeste. *The Life and Letters of Peter Ilich Tchaikovsky*. New York: Haskell House, 1970.

Tolman, Edward Chace. *Purposive Behavior in Animals and Men*. New York: Appleton-Century-Crofts, 1932.

Tolstoy, Leo. *Recollections and Essays*. New York: Oxford University Press, 1937.

Van Doren, Charles. "Mathematics." In *The Paideia Program*. Edited by Mortimer Adler. New York: Macmillan, 1984.

Walzer, John F. "A Period of Ambivalence: Eighteenth-Century American Childhood." In *The History of Childhood*. Edited by Lloyd deMause. New York: Psychohistory Press, 1974.

Watson, John B. "An Attempted Formulation of the Scope of Behavior Psychology." *Psychological Review* 24 (September 1917): 329–52.

———. *Behaviorism*. 1924. Reprint, Chicago: University of Chicago Press, 1961.

———. "The Place of the Conditioned Reflex in Psychology." *Psychological Review* 23 (March 1916): 89–117.

———. "Practical and Theoretical Problems in Instinct and Habit." In *Suggestions of Modern Science Concerning Education*. Edited by H. S. Jennings et al. New York: Macmillan, 1917.

———. "Psychology as the Behaviorist Views It." *Psychological Review* 20 (March 1913): 158–77.

———. *Psychology from the Standpoint of a Behaviorist*. Philadelphia: J. B. Lippincott, 1919.

Watson, John B., and J. J. B. Morgan. "Emotional Reactions and Psychological Experimentation." *American Journal of Psychology* 28 (1917): 163–74.

Watson, John B., and Rosalie Rayner. "Conditioned Emotional Reactions." *Journal of Experimental Psychology* 3 (1920): 1–14.

Watson, John B., and Rosalie R. Watson. *Psychological Care of Infant and Child*. New York: W. W. Norton, 1928.

Wilde, Oscar. *The Soul of Man under Socialism*. In *The Works of Oscar Wilde*. New York: P. F. Collier & Son, 1927.

Wilson, Edwin, ed. *Shaw on Shakespeare*. New York: E. P. Dutton, 1961.

Yawkey, Thomas D., ed. *The Self-Concept of the Young Child*. Provo, Utah: Brigham Young University Press, 1980.

Zweig, Stefan. *The World of Yesterday*. Lincoln: University of Nebraska Press, 1964.

Index

Adams, Solomon, 105
Adler, Mortimer, 36, 103
Allen, James E. Jr., 92–93
Authoritarianism
  of German schooling, 88
  of Mann, 92
  of Piaget's interaction with children,
    23–25
  from pseudoscience, 90–93

Barker, Stephen, 37
Behaviorist theory
  of Hull, 6
  influence on educators, 6–7
  law of conditioning (Skinner), 16
  of Skinner, 16–18
  of Watson, 6–16
Bestor, Arthur, 66
Boaz, David, 95–96, 100–101, 112
Boole, George, 22
Boyer, Ernest, 29–33, 39–40, 96
Brecht, Arnold, 28
Broad, C. D., 24
Bruner, Jerome
  MACOS class of, 71–76, 106
  on memorizing, 79
  on shaping children, 85, 103
  structuralist theory, 68–69

Carnegie Foundation for the
  Advancement of Teaching, 29, 72
Center for Cognitive Studies, Harvard
  University, 68
Chess, Stella, 105
Children
  Bruner's structuralist theory, 68–69
  control of (Mann), 92
  development of logical thinking
    (Piaget), 19–21
  differences and different needs of,
    98–99, 104–13
  directing reading of, 48–59
  education according to Owen, 91
  educators' ideas of shaping, 85

expected behavior under progressive
  ideas, 67
forced memorizing, 79
forced to learn to read, 43–44
improvement of reading speed,
  44–48
knowledge tests for (Ravitch, Finn),
  56
learning to read, 43
Mann's approach to shaping of,
  88–89
Mann's view of authoritarian control
  of, 92
Piaget's interaction with, 23–25
problem-solving process (Boyer),
  39–40
proposed psychosocial treatment for,
  92–93
role in schooling (Mann), 88
in science of society, 89
17th-century perception of, 85–86
training minds of (Mann), 5
Chomsky, Noam, 16–17, 80, 93
Colfax, David, 103, 109–10
Colfax, Micki, 103, 109–10
Combe, George, 5
Committee on Economy of Time in
  Education, 67
Communication
  elements of human, 53–54
  factors in good, 53–55
  relation to knowledge (Ravitch,
    Finn), 53
Competition among schools, 97–110
Comte, Auguste, 90
Conant, James B., 1
Condorcet, M. J., 89
Consciousness, Piaget's concept of, 24
Curriculum
  in homeschooling, 109
  progressive, 65–66
  of public school, 103
  structuralist, 69–76
  See also Mathematics curriculum

Dana, Richard Henry Jr., 57–58
deMause, Lloyd, 86
Dennett, Daniel, 17–18
Dewey, John, 64, 85
Dickens, Charles, 51
du Pont, Pete, 98–99, 104

Education
    Committee on Economy of Time in
        Education, 67
    Emerson's view of, 61
    life-adjustment, 65
    Mann's idea of, 5
    Owen's idea of, 91
    progressive movement in, 63–68
    in science of society, 89–90
    structuralist movement in, 68–77
    theory related to cultural literacy,
        79–83
    theory related to mathematics, 36
    See also Schooling process
Educational Excellence Network, 49, 54
Education Commission of the States, 98
Education reform
    progressivism, 63–68
    structuralism, 68–77
    See also Homeschooling; School
        choice
Educators
    advocacy of prescribed reading,
        48–53
    claims for mathematics curriculum,
        42
    conception of individuality, 104–6
    improving communication ability,
        54–56
    influence of behaviorism on, 6–7, 15
    rhetoric of, 27
    view of memorizing, 79
Einstein, Albert, 39, 112
Elkind, David, 43
Emerson, Ralph Waldo, 51, 61

Feynman, Richard, 70–71
Fichte, Johann Gottlieb, 88
Finn, Chester, 49–51, 53, 56–59
Friedman, Milton, 97, 98, 100

In re Gault, 107
Goodman, Paul, 106–7
Gould, Glenn, 52
Gwartney, James, 95

Hartley, Mariette, 15

Hayek, Friedrich, 46
Hefferman, Helen, 44
Hirsch, E. D. Jr.
    on choices of children's reading,
        54–55
    cultural literacy concept, 79–80
    fact list, 81–83
    on memorizing, 79
Hofstadter, Richard, 65
Holt, John, 20–21, 39
Homeschooling
    approach to children with, 108–9
    curriculum, 109
Honig, Bill, 96
Hull, Clark, 6
Hutchins, Robert, 106

Illinois Curriculum Program, 65–66
Individualism (Wilde), 112
Individuality
    of children, 104
    public school conception of, 104–5
Intelligence
    Piaget's theory of development of, 19
    relation to reading, 43
Introspectionism, 6–7

James, William, 7

Kessler, Harry Graf, 28–29, 32
Kilpatrick, William Heard, 64
Kline, Morris, 35, 37–38, 40, 74
Knowledge
    basis for (Hayek), 46
    educators' claims of scientific, 3, 5–6
    relation to communication (Ravitch,
        Finn), 53–57
    schooling based on scientific (Mann),
        1–2, 5
Kolderie, Ted, 97

Law of conditioning (Skinner), 16
Learning
    behaviorists' theory, 6–18
    Holt's view of children's, 39
    meaningful, 106–7
    progressivism's scientific laws of,
        64–67
    to read, 43–44, 60–62
Lebowitz, Fran, 35–36
Leibniz, Gottfried Wilhelm von, 22
LeShan, Eda, 47, 110–11
Lichtenberg, Georg Christoph, 46
Lieberman, Myron, 98

Life-adjustment education, 65
Locke, John, 86–87
Logic, propositional (Piaget), 19–24
Lynd, Albert, 66

McDonald, Kay, 105
"Man: A Course of Study" (MACOS),
    71–76
Mann, Horace
    claims for schooling process, 1–2
    concept of schooling, 88, 102
    on crime prevention, 110
    idea of authoritarian control, 92
    idea of schooling process, 27–29, 33
    ideas related to phrenology, 90
    ideas to shape children, 85, 89
    list of suitable books, 57–58
    premise of children's sameness,
        104–5
    schooling based on scientific laws, 5,
        89
Maslow, Abraham, 105
Mathematics
    childrens' study of, 35
    contradictions in, 37–38
    perceptions of mathematicians
        (Pascal), 41
    structuralists' view, 68–71
    thinking in actual study of, 40
Mathematics curriculum
    Boyer's defense of, 39–40
    educators' argument for, 42
    new math concept, 69–71
    Van Doren's defense of, 36–37, 40
Matthews, Gareth, 24–25
Memorizing, rote (Hirsch), 79–80
Mencken, H. L., 48, 60
Meredith, George, 51
Messerli, Jonathan, 92, 104–5
Mill, John Stuart, 97–98, 104
Moore, Dorothy, 43–44, 60
Moore, Raymond, 43–44, 60

Nietzche, Friedrich, 51, 52

Owen, Robert, 91–92, 102

Paideia Group, 36, 103
Pascal, Blaise, 41
Pavlov, Ivan, 7
Peters, R. S., 6
Phrenology
    as basis for education (Mann), 5–6,
        18

Combe's theory of, 5
Comte's "science" of, 90
Piaget, Jean
    interaction with children, 23–25
    scientific theory of, 19–26
Pope, Alexander, 53
Problem-solving process (Boyer), 39–40
Progressive Education Association, 64
Progressivism in education, 63–68, 76
Project Method, 64–65
Psychology
    behaviorist theory of learning, 18
    behaviorist theory (Skinner), 16–18
    behaviorist theory (Watson), 6–16
    introspectionism, 6–7
Psychosocial treatment, 92–93

Radner, Gilda, 59
Ravitch, Diane, 49–51, 53, 56–59
Reading
    developing speed, 44–48
    educators' distortion of role of, 62
    learning to read, 60
    prescribed, 48–53, 55–60, 62
    schools' approach to, 43
Reinforcement (Skinner), 16
Respect (Emerson), 61
Russell, Bertrand, 9, 23, 38

Saint-Simon, Henri, 89–90
School choice
    arguments against, 100–102
    arguments for, 98–99
    competition with, 97–110
    See also Voucher plan
Schooling process
    dissatisfaction with, 1
    educational rhetoric describing, 27
    Mann's concept of, 1–2, 27–29, 88, 92
    Piaget's theory, 19–22
    See also Homeschooling
Schools
    argument against privatizing, 100
    authoritarian private, 107
    as clinics, 92
    competing, 97–110
    progressive reforms, 63–68
    structuralist reforms, 68–77
Schools, German
    criticism of, 28–29
    Mann's rhetoric related to, 27–29, 33
    Zweig's description, 33–34
Schools, public
    actual offerings, 103

conception of children's
individuality, 104–5
criticism of, 95–98
lack of curriculum, 103
Mann's claims for, 1–2
reading in, 60
School system
as bureaucratic monopoly, 95–97
with choice and competition, 97–104
German, 88
Science, educational
of Piaget, 22
of progressivism, 63–68
of structuralism, 68–77
Science of society (Condorcet), 89–90
Scientific laws
of mental development (Mann), 5, 89,
92
of progressivism, 64–67
Shakespeare, William, 52, 54
Shanker, Albert, 96
Shaw, George Bernard, 52
Silberman, Charles, 2, 26, 32, 110
Skinner, B. F., 16–18
Smith, Nila Banton, 44–47
Social studies, structuralists' view,
71–76
Society
Owen's view of, 91
science of (Condorcet), 89–90
Stevenson, Robert Louis, 52
Structuralism in education, 68–76
Students. See Children

Swinburne, Algernon, 51

Tchaikovsky, Peter I., 52
Teachers
as learning clinicians, 92–93
role of (Mann), 88
Teacher's College, Columbia
University, 64, 65
Teaching, Piaget's theory, 2
Thinking
Einstein's view of, 39
mathematical, 41–42
in study of mathematics, 40–42
Thinking, rational
Piaget's theory of, 19–20, 28
Van Doren's view, 38–39
Thomas, Alexander, 105
Thoreau, Henry David, 51–52
Tolman, Edward Chace, 14–15
Tolstoy, Leo, 52

Van Doren, Charles, 36–40
Vico, Giambattista, 41
Voucher plan, 98–100

Watson, John B., 6, 8–16
Watson, Rosalie Rayner, 15
Western civilization course (Boyer),
29–32
Whitehead, Alfred North, 23
Wilde, Oscar, 112

Zweig, Stefan, 33–34

About the Author

Bruce Goldberg is a professor of philosophy at the University of Maryland. His articles have appeared in numerous journals including *Philosophical Studies, Analysis* and *American Philosophical Quarterly*. He has also contributed to several volumes of essays on issues in the philosophy of mind and the philosophy of language.

Cato Institute

Founded in 1977, the Cato Institute is a public policy research foundation dedicated to broadening the parameters of policy debate to allow consideration of more options that are consistent with the traditional American principles of limited government, individual liberty, and peace. To that end, the Institute strives to achieve greater involvement of the intelligent, concerned lay public in questions of policy and the proper role of government.

The Institute is named for *Cato's Letters,* libertarian pamphlets that were widely read in the American Colonies in the early 18th century and played a major role in laying the philosophical foundation for the American Revolution.

Despite the achievement of the nation's Founders, today virtually no aspect of life is free from government encroachment. A pervasive intolerance for individual rights is shown by government's arbitrary intrusions into private economic transactions and its disregard for civil liberties.

To counter that trend, the Cato Institute undertakes an extensive publications program that addresses the complete spectrum of policy issues. Books, monographs, and shorter studies are commissioned to examine the federal budget, Social Security, regulation, military spending, international trade, and myriad other issues. Major policy conferences are held throughout the year, from which papers are published thrice yearly in the *Cato Journal.* The Institute also publishes the quarterly magazine *Regulation.*

In order to maintain its independence, the Cato Institute accepts no government funding. Contributions are received from foundations, corporations, and individuals, and other revenue is generated from the sale of publications. The Institute is a nonprofit, tax-exempt, educational foundation under Section 501(c)3 of the Internal Revenue Code.

CATO INSTITUTE
1000 Massachusetts Ave., N.W.
Washington, D.C. 20001